I0118338

ITALIANS IN FLORIDA

GARY R. MORMINO

BORDIGHERA PRESS

NEW YORK, NEW YORK

Library of Congress Control Number: 2008928367

with grateful acknowledgement to the Consulate of Italy in Miami

© 2008 by Gary Mormino

All rights reserved. Parts of this book may be reprinted only by written permission from the authors, and may not be reproduced for publication in book, magazine, or electronic media of any kind, except in quotations for purposes of literary reviews by critics.

Printed in the United States.

Published by
BORDIGHERA PRESS
John D. Calandra Italian American Institute
25 West 43rd Street, 17th Floor
New York, NY 10036

VIA FOLIOS 51
ISBN 1–884419–97–6

To Sara Guarino and Rosolino Mormino,
grandparents whom I barely knew,
and to my father, Ross Anthony Mormino,
the hardest working man I have ever known,
whose sacrifices made the American Dream possible.

TABLE OF CONTENTS

Author's Preface

From New Spain across the Old South to the New South, from Dream State to the Sunbelt, Italians have figured prominently in the history of Florida. From the earliest Spanish voyages of exploration to the massive migration of second- and third-generation ethnics after World War II, Italians have witnessed and participated in the extraordinary transformation of America's southernmost state.

What follows is an overview of the history of Italians in Florida. What will become apparent is that Florida's growth and development as a state is inextricably tied to the history of Italians in this part of the United States, the one would be different today without the other.

Because my primary audience is a more general reading public, and because I have provided a bibliography of books and articles at the end of this book, I have decided not to interrupt the reading with footnotes or page references. The reader will find all s/he needs in the appended list of references.

Explorers and Colonists

On October 12, 1492, the Genovese-born navigator Cristóforo Colombo stepped ashore on a wind-swept island in the Bahamas. This simple act set in motion a series of revolutions still being felt today. The most important event of 1492 was not discovery—the Native Americans had long resided in the place that Europeans "discovered." The most significant consequence was the encounter between Europeans and Americans, the beginning of the "Columbian Exchange," the profound interplay and interchange of microbes, foodstuffs, animals, and ideas amongst the world's peoples. Lest we forget, before 1492, no Italian had ever sampled *pasta con pomodori, gnocchi, polenta,* or *cioccolato.*

Colombo, better known by his hispanicized and anglicized names, Cristóbal Colón and Christopher Columbus, also ignited the European movement to discover and colonize the New World. Historians still dispute who first set sight upon the place called Florida today. Some insist Italian-born navigators Giovanni di Verrazzano or the Cabot brothers accomplished the feat. Amerigo Vespucci's map, in turn, gave a name to the new continent, America.

Italians played instrumental roles in New Spain, especially in the fields of navigation and commerce. Significant numbers of Italians—principally Genoans, Ligurians, and Florentines—sought for-

Columbus Statue at Port Everglades, Fort Lauderdale, Florida; 12 October 1992. Courtesy of Frank J. Cavaioli.

tunes in Spain and its empire. Emperor Charles V and succeeding Spanish kings ruled parts of the Italian peninsula and islands. "Italians," wrote the historian Lyle M. McCalister, "particularly Genoese, living in the principal commercial centers of the Indies made up the second largest identifiable foreign element (following the Portuguese)."

Italians were especially prized for their map-making skills. In the most secret room of Seville, Spain, cartographers scrutinized ship logs and sea charts of returning voyagers. At some point early in the sixteenth century, as more information came in weekly of new exploration, a spit of land jutting into the Caribbean was identified as part of a great continent.

The first recorded exploration of this mysterious place occurred in 1513 when Juan Ponce de León, the governor of Puerto Rico and the steely *conquistador* of the Bahamas, embarked on an ambitious expedition. In 1512, King Ferdinand of Spain rewarded Ponce de León with a *capitulácion* [royal license] to discover new lands. The motivation was part fantasy, part profit. Caribbean Indians had spread rumors of a Fountain of Youth. Accounts of such a place appeared in the works of a remarkable Italian cleric, Pietro Martire d'Anghiera (Peter Martyr). Leaving Italy in 1497 to serve the court of Ferdinand and Isabella as a resident scholar of the humanities, he truly understood the magnitude of the events unfolding before him. He mentioned a place in the New World the Natives called "the Springs of Bimini, a River in Florida." Where magical springs miraculously made old men young, the infertile fertile, and the infirmed healthy, but also where mountains of gold and Native slave labor were believed to exist, Ponce de León sailed from Puerto Rico on March 3, 1513, in three ships, "well provided with food, men, and mariners." The expedition also included two women and one "Jorge Negro." The captain of Ponce's flagship was an Italian identified as Juan or Giovanni Bono.

The voyagers sighted land after a month at sea. According to court historian Antonio Herrera, "Believing the land to be an island, they named it *La Florida,* because it appeared very delightful, having many fresh groves and because they discovered it at the season the Spaniards called *Pascua Florida* [the flowers of Easter] . . . they went ashore to take possession."

"Florida," rhapsodized the poet Elizabeth Bishop in 1946, "The state with the prettiest name. . . ." *La Florida!*—what a splendid name for a place bedecked with flowers and dreams. For Juan Ponce de León, *La Florida* would also become his nightmare. He returned in 1521, hoping to establish a colony. Alas, off the southwest coast of what is today's Pine Island or Sanibel Island, Calusa Indians drove the Spaniards away, inflicting a grievous, mortal wound upon the leader.

A succession of explorers returned to *La Florida.* Italians accompanied the Spanish and French in the early expeditions. The grandest *entrada* of them all was the Hernando de Soto expedition. In 1539, de Soto, the conqueror of the Incas, landed at Tampa Bay with an armed force of nearly 600 men, 223 horses, dozens of pigs, and provisions for an invasion. Included was Captain Cristóbal Espindola, a native of Genoa and a relative of Cabeza de Vaca, the treasurer. Espindola was entrusted with the sixty halberdiers of de Soto's personal guard. Francisco Aceituono, a Genoese engineer, and two unnamed caulkers, one a Genoan, the other a Sardinian, also participated in the adventure. Following de Soto's death, Maestro Francisco took charge building seven brigantines that allowed the survivors to sail down the Mississippi River.

In 1565, King Philip II of Spain dispatched Pedro Menéndez de Avilés, the Captain General of the West Indies Fleet, to drive the French out of Florida. Menéndez ruthlessly put the French Protestants to the sword, destroyed the Huguenot settlement at Fort Caroline on the St. Johns River, and founded the city of San Agustín, named for the great Saint Augustine. The chaplain of the Menéndez expedition left an account of the events. His report mentioned that when the Spanish first sighted land, "an Italian boy of nine went ashore looking for water." The young man is later identified as a Lombard.

Individual Italians worked in various capacities throughout Florida's First Spanish Period, 1565–1763. Italians served as Jesuit missionaries, working among the mission villages. Italians were employed as engineers in the construction of El Castillo de San Marcos, soldiers in the king's army, and pirates marauding silver fleets (Nicoló Strozzi). A popular Spanish saying insisted, "No hay hombre bajo el sol como el Italiano y el Español." [There is no man under the sun like the Italian and the Spaniard.] The first Italian born in what became the continental United States was almost certainly Francisco de Florencia. Born in St. Augustine in 1620, de Florencia (a Florentine) became a Jesuit priest in 1643. Numerous Italian-born clerics traveled to Florida. The first evidence of a definite Italian presence in Florida is offered by a Dec. 22, 1736 communication from Fray Francisco, the Bishop of Santiago, Cuba, to the Governor of Cuba. He wrote, "There is also an Italian store, permanently located."

The oldest document in the Florida State Archives depicts Sir Francis Drake's May 1586 raid on Spanish St. Augustine. The hand-colored map and engraving was the work of the Italian cartographer Baptista Boazio.

John Wesley preached in Florida and Georgia in 1736–1737. The founder of Methodism learned Spanish for his foray into Florida, where he described meeting Italians in his journal. By the end of the eighteenth century, a half dozen Italian stores had been established in St. Augustine. The Spanish census of 1786 confirms this Italian presence, although most Italian names have been hispanicized (Giuseppe to José, Paolo to Pablo, Giovanni to Juan, etc.).

Florida thus became one of the great pathways to North America, and one of the great meeting grounds on the planet, a place where Europeans, Africans, Native Americans, and people from the Caribbean and South America met and melded new cultures. Italians were present at the creation.

British Florida: Time of Sorrows

In 1763, Spain's misfortunes in The Seven Years War (in America, called The French and Indian War) reverberated in Florida. British successes on land and sea across several continents reaped diplomatic and imperial fruits. British and Spanish diplomats engineered an exchange, essentially swapping the captured port city of Havana, Cuba, for *La Florida*. Thus the period 1763 to 1783 is known as British Florida. During the American Revolution, East and West Florida—the so-called Fourteenth Colony, chose to remain loyal to the Crown. Only a few thousand Europeans inhabited this isolated and vast section of Florida, outnumbered by the Natives and African slaves.

Italians figured in one of the most sensational episodes of the era. "Florida fever" swept the British Isles as the second sons of landed gentry looked for fresh and exotic places to earn fortunes denied their birthright. Literary tracts painted British Florida as an Edenic paradise, a land begging for the cultivation of rice, cotton and sugar, indigo and olive trees.

Such lofty and rhapsodic passages caught the attention of a Scottish-born physician. Dr. Andrew Turnbull had established a reputation as a world traveler, spending several years as a surgeon in the Ottoman Empire. He obtained a generous tract of 20,000 acres in British East Florida at a site ominously named Mosquito Inlet (in today's Volusia County). Convinced that "white" indentured servants could clear the Florida wilderness and turn a profit, Turnbull scoured the Mediterranean for recruits in the spring of 1768. Married to an Italian-born Levantine, he was unsuccessful at convincing Italian silk-worm cultivators to come to America. He then went to the Italian Leghorn, Greece, and the Belaric Islands off Spain's eastern coast (then controlled by England). He eventually convinced 1,403 persons to pledge seven years of labor in exchange for passage to Florida. Workers included Greeks, Minorcans, and Italians (110 in total, chiefly Ligurian, but from across the peninsula). Turnbull figured that a diverse workforce would not likely rebel or unite.

Following a harrowing ocean voyage, the seven ships of sorrows arrived on the East Coast of Florida. The site must have been hauntingly beautiful: mangrove swamps, vast pine barrens, the winding Hillsborough River, and a large bluff where the settlers were expected to carve out a new life. Calling this new place New Smyrna—after his wife's beloved Smyrna in Turkey—Turnbull ordered the hapless settlers to clear the land of the tough palmetto vegetation, plant crops, and build shelters. An African slave ship had sunk, depriving Turnbull of laborers. Heartbroken that neither the vine nor olive nor artichoke flourished in humid Florida, the workers made the best of this strange new land. Turnbull was gambling that his cash crop, indigo, would bring a handsome profit. The indigo plant yields a deep violet blue dye, valuable in the textile trade.

The indigo plantation proved to be a commercial failure, but not as catastrophic as the human tragedy unfolding at New Smyrna. The settlement became a death camp; fully a quarter of the workers died in the first six months. Half of the original settlers would not last more than two years. Bedeviled by voracious mosquitoes, tormented by brutal overseers, the Greeks, Minorcans, and Italians rebelled in August 1768. The rebellion was ruthlessly crushed when two of the loyal Italian overseers alerted Turnbull. Italians seem to have instigated the rebellion. Governor James Grant ordered the insurgents be taken to St. Augustine for trial. Three Italians were condemned to death: Carlo Forni (the alleged ringleader and so-called "first martyr of Italian labor in America"), Giuseppi Massiadoli (who cut off two fingers and an ear of an English driver identified as Mr. Cutter), and a Corsican, Elia Medici (for killing a cow). The British surveyor Bernard Romans witnessed the proceedings. He described the execution:

> Elia Medici was obliged to be executioner of Massiadoli and Forni. On this occasion I saw one of the most moving scenes I ever experienced: long and obstinate was the struggle of this man's mind, who repeatedly called out, that he chose to die rather than be executioner of his friends in distress . . . till at length the entreaties of the victims themselves, put an end to the conflict in his breast, by encouraging him to the act. Now we beheld a man thus compelled to mount the ladder, take leave of his friends in the most moving manner, kissing them the moment before he committed them to an ignominious death.

The New Smyrna experiment was doomed. Eventually several hundred survivors made their way to British St. Augustine, a town already celebrating its 200th anniversary. There, several dozen Italians carved out a niche in the "Ancient City." They integrated into the town's polyglot mixture. Many of the Italian men had already married Spanish and Greek women. In 1787, Governor Manuel de Zéspedes unflatteringly described the remnants of New Smyrna to a royal official: "The present population of this country . . . 488 Minorcans, Italians, and Greeks. . . . Their sloth compels me to inform your Excellency that they are nothing but a useless expense to the royal treasury."

The names of the survivors, especially Italians, were altered and Minorcinized (Pacetti became Pacetty; Trotti became Troti; Maestri became Mastry). Gradually, the Italians adapted to and were assimilated by the pervasive Minorcan and Spanish society. They would largely be misidentified as Minorcans; their children would be *Criolles* or Creoles, the American-born children of emigrants.

Every immigrant generation reminds the next of the ordeal of emigration and the travail of adjustment, but few matched the harrowing saga of eighteenth-century New Smyrna. British St. Augustine still contained descendents of Spanish Florida. Florida was underpopulated and the Italians provided much needed labor and energy. Italians could have found few places in America more receptive to their religion and nativity than the small settlement in northeast Florida. Names, such as Antonio Berta, a wine merchant in St. Augustine, endure as entries in dusty archives.

One of the most interesting Italians in late eighteenth-century Florida was surely Maria Magdalena Crespel, the daughter of Oreste Crespel of Nice, France, who could speak six languages. She married don Francisco Felipe Fatio, the owner of New Switzerland, a vast plantation and cattle ranch in British East Florida located on the St. Johns River. The Fatios remained on their plantation when Spain returned to power in Florida in 1783. Maria died a *Floridana* in St. Augustine in 1810.

An anonymous writer left this intriguing document about life in 1819 St. Augustine. "They (Italians) are honest, simple and laborious in their occupations as fishermen and farmers. They forcibly brought before me the scenes and sounds of sunny Italy."

The 1820 Spanish Census of Pensacola documents a handful of Italian-born residents: Timia Deslinio, storekeeper; Desiderio Quina, storekeeper; Recio Dominga, a billiard parlor operator from Genoa; Ariolo Cristóbal, carpenter; and Antonio Raismundo, guide. It is unclear whether these Italian-born residents of Spanish West Florida chose to remain in Pensacola when the city and territory changed hands a few years later as the United States acquired Florida.

Royalty

The most romantic and intriguing Italian in nineteenth-century Florida, perhaps America, was undoubtedly Charles Louis Napoléon Achille Murat, the Crown Prince of Naples. Few Floridians have ever traveled such a life's journey from perfumed European parlors to the rustic red hills of North Florida. Achille's uncle was none other than Napoleon Bonaparte, the Corsican who would be emperor; his father was the dashing General Joachim Murat, the hero of the Egyptian campaign, the King of Naples.

Napoleon's empire was crushed at Waterloo in 1815. A period of repression and restoration followed. Napoleon spent the rest of his life in exile at Helena, while a firing squad dispatched the King of Naples. Prince Murat's life was saved only because of a delicious turn of fate: the iron hand of reactionary Prince Metternich of Austria spared the young man because he had once had an affair with Queen Caroline, Murat's mother. Young Achille joined Queen Caroline in sanctuary at an Austrian castle, but at age 23, he bolted for America.

Achille Murat sailed from Europe and landed in St. Augustine. The exiled prince, after a brief and unpleasant stay in East Florida, settled in Leon County to live the life of a gentleman farmer. He purchased a thousand-acre plantation west of Tallahassee, which he named Lipona, after his mother, who had become the Countess of Lipona (an anagram of Napoli) in exile. His plantation home was modest, even for a deposed prince. Lipona consisted of a one-room log cabin. Murat adored his adopted country, writing, "It is the American Union that gives the best model of government."

His 1826 marriage to a 23-year-old-widow, Catherine Willis Gray, the great-grand niece of George Washington caused quite a stir; indeed, many tongues wagged that widow Gray was marrying down. Indeed, Murat's personal habits reinforced his image as a very odd man. Friends detected that he seldom if ever bathed or changed his clothes; moreover, he was a notorious womanizer and used his dog as a spittoon. He also demonstrated a fascination with local fowl and game, a willingness to consume roasted owl, buzzard, and hawk. He lost a finger in a sensational duel with a local judge, an ironic twist considering he was later appointed a territorial judge. The Panic of 1837 wiped out his modest assets, and he was never able to retrieve his family's fortune in Europe. He died in poverty in 1847. The graves of Achille and Catherine Murat, marked by stone obelisks, rest at St. John's Cemetery, a short stroll from the campus of Florida State University in Tallahassee.

Frontier Florida

One of the survivors of the New Smyrna debacle was Joseph Bonelli, a native of Livorno, Italy. He escaped to St. Augustine and by 1802 was residing on a six-hundred-acre estate on the south side of the Bar of Matanzas, an inlet near St. Augustine. The name Matanzas means massacre in Spanish and denotes the place Catholics put to the sword French heretics in 1565. In 1802, the Bonelli *hacienda* was attacked by Miccosukee Indians. The Indians burned his plantation and carried off several family members. Several Bonelly (the spelling has changed) sons and daughters survived the captivity.

British rule of Florida lasted only twenty years. At the Treaty of Paris, American delegates wanted nothing to do with a strong British presence south of the newly formed United States, and thus, Spain returned to the peninsula. The Second Spanish Period, however, was also short lived. Imperial Spain, once the most formidable power in the world, had overextended Spanish resources and squandered New World riches. Spain encouraged St. Augustine's Latin citizens to remain. Italians who pledged loyalty to the Spanish Crown remained. In 1821, Congress ratified the Adams-Onís Treaty, ceding Florida to the United States. A new chapter of Italian-American activity began.

American officials discovered the newest US Territory a very strange place. Vestiges of Creole culture and pockets of ethnicity existed in the two principal cities of Pensacola and St. Augustine. When Rachel Jackson, the prudish and opinionated wife of General Andrew Jackson, arrived at the West Florida port city of Pensacola in 1821, she was horrified. "The inhabitants all speak Spanish and French. Some speak four languages!" she confessed. "Such a mixed multitude . . . fish peddlers filling the street with incomprehensible cries. . . ."

Fort Brooke, founded in 1824, marked the beginnings of modern Tampa. The military outpost located at the confluence of the Hillsborough River and Hillsborough Bay, served as a major gathering point for soldiers and settlers who dared penetrate the South Florida frontier. Pensacola and Key West acquired naval stations. Fort Lauderdale, Fort Myers, and Fort Ogden began as military installations during the Indian Wars. A small number of Italians enlisted in the Second (1837–1842) and Third (1855–1857) Seminole Wars. William Banta, captain in the US Navy, died at Indian Key in 1842. John Netto, an officer's steward in the navy, died at Pensacola in 1838. Little is known about Privates E.P. Allanti, G.F. Alberte, John Camba, David Pinto, and Joseph Tessore, who spent time at Fort Brooke in the 1840s, and may or may not have been Italian.

Nineteenth-Century Wars

Between 1770 and 1870, St. Augustine may have been the most Italian city in America, although Italians quickly deferred to British, Minorcan, Spanish, and American rule and custom. Vestiges of *italianitá* survived. Italians, by dint of survival and intermarriage, became part and parcel of the Ancient City's social and economic fabric. When the Civil War began, G. Antonio Pacetti was mayor of St. Augustine. When Union troops captured the city, Pacetti defiantly refused to surrender, choosing a blockade-runner to Cuba to dishonor.

By 1860, the Italians of St. Augustine had raised three, even four, generations and had deep roots. Their response to the clarion call of the Civil War reveals their commitment to their new home. Scores of Italian Americans enlisted in the Third and Eighth Infantries, comprised of citizens of St. Johns County. Their stories add a remarkable chapter to our history.

First Lt. Joseph Anthony Pacetti was born in St. Augustine in 1839. A graduate of the University of Maryland, he practiced medicine in St. Augustine before the war. He was captured at the battle of Fredericksburg in December 1862, and paroled in a prisoner exchange. He returned to service but resigned in November 1864 after being elected to the Florida Legislature. After the war, Pacetti lived and worked in Cuba and Jacksonville.

The war produced family heroes and legends. Edward Ambrose Papy, a native of St. Augustine, enlisted in the Third Florida Infantry in July 1862. Brothers Isadore and Joseph served by his side. Edward was wounded at Perryville, captured and then exchanged in a prisoner swap at Vicksburg. He was fatally wounded at Sayler's Creek in April 1865. Brother Isadore served as a drummer and was promoted to chief musician. After the war he made his fortune in Georgia and Alabama. A monument in St. Augustine honors the brothers' sacrifices.

In 1849, ship's captain Domenico Ghira arrived in Tampa. A native of Ravenna, then part of the Austro-Hungarian Empire, he became Tampa's first permanent Italian citizen. In 1850, he married Domenica Maestri. In 1853 Ghira became a US citizen. Ghira enlisted in the Florida militia and fought in the Billy Bowlegs War, the last Indian uprising east of the Mississippi. Ghira went on to become a very successful ship captain and real estate holder. One of his many civic responsibilities included operating the Hillsborough River Ferry. When Ghira died in 1897, he owned substantial holdings in what became downtown Tampa.

The Maestri family branched out from New Smyrna and St. Augustine to become cattlemen, or in the Florida vernacular, "cow-hunters." Pablo Maestri was listed in 1800 as a surgeon of the 3rd Battalion of Cuban Infantry stationed in St. Augustine. They also fought in several Indian Wars. Some are now known as Masters, having anglicized the name. In a similar fashion, the Tagliaferro family gradually changed its name to Taliaferro and then Tolliver.

Italians fought for the Union and Confederacy during the Civil War. Bancroft Gherardi commanded several Union Blockade ships off the coast of Florida and later became chief and admiral of the North Atlantic Squadron.

Francisco Bartolo Papy lived a remarkable life. Born in St. Augustine in 1838, he fought in the Third Seminole War and then served in the Civil War, enlisting in the Second Florida Infantry in Tallahassee. Decorated at the Battle of Olustee, the most significant engagement fought in Florida, he was discharged as a Sgt. Major. He lost a brother in the war. After the war he worked for the Plant System Railroad. He died in 1903.

The Civil War also produced its share of controversies, of which Italian Americans participated. Herbert Pacetti was one of many soldiers to desert. In 1863, Herbert Pacetti, Isadore Papy, and Andrew Canova were tried and convicted of stealing provisions from a Tennessee farmer. The men were sentenced to six months of hard labor. Canova, an Indian War hero, deserted.

In the spring of 1862, Federal troops seized St. Augustine, a symbolic victory. S.F. DuPont, flag officer aboard the *USS Wabash*, dispatched a report to Gideon Welles, Secretary of the Navy, expressing concern about the civilians of the newly occupied city.

> There is much violent and pestilent feeling among the women. They seem to mistake treason for courage and have a theatrical desire to figure as heroines. On the night before our arrival, a party of women assembled in front of the barracks and cut down the flagstaff, in order that it might be used to support the old flag.

On April 12, 1862, authorities, exasperated at the civil unrest, placed St. Augustine under martial law. In May, an officer complained in a report, "A party of young ladies assembled in the Plaza and commenced chipping off small pieces from the stump of the old flag staff, which they kissed with the fervor of a youthful maiden in her first love." Enraged by such behavior, Lt. Col. Louis Ball of the 4th New Hampshire Volunteers, banished scores of women from the city who had been abusive *and* had husbands in the Confederate forces. Among those exiled were Pamphilia Masters, Monica Masters Genovar, Mary Louise Leonardy, and the wife and three children of Joseph Capo.

Andrew Canova survived two wars to write his autobiography in 1885. Credit: Special Collections, University of South Florida.

For a life of sheer adventure, few nineteenth-century figures could match Andrew P. Canova. Born in 1835, he must have heard about New Smyrna firsthand from the last survivors of the fiasco. In his early twenties, Canova enlisted to fight in the Third Seminole or Billy Bowlegs War, 1855–1858. He poled across the eddies and bayous of the Florida interior, shooting wild hogs on Sanibel Island, hunting Seminole Chief Billy Bowlegs, and marching through the trackless Everglades. In one episode, he lost a thumb in the jaws of a soft shell turtle. On another occasion, he and his company were sleeping on a bank of a Florida stream. During the night, one of the men awoke screaming. Hundreds of large alligators had crawled onto the camp site, attracted by the odors of cooking food (and humans). He survived, only to enlist in the Civil War. Following the war, he became a successful businessman. He wrote a series of newspaper articles about his military exploits for the *Palatka Southern Sun*. In 1885, the essays were published as *Life and Adventures in South Florida: Reminiscences of a Trip Through the Everglades During the Last Indian War*. Canova Beach on Florida's East Coast honors his legacy.

The Papy/Papi family also achieved fame during this era. Arriving in Tampa in 1848, Antonio Papi was the descendent of Gaspar Papi and Anna Pons of St. Augustine. After heroic service in the Confederacy, Papi moved across Tampa Bay and homesteaded along the Pinellas peninsula. Papy's Bayou at Weedon Island honors his fishing *rancho* he had established on Tampa Bay.

Joseph B. Papy was born in St. Augustine in 1831. A veteran of the Third Seminole War—he served as a bugler—he worked as a butcher and saddler. He enlisted in the Third Florida Infantry. Promoted to musician and then drum major, he was assigned to a saddle factory in Columbus, Georgia. He died in Florida in 1911.

The family name Pacetty/Pacetti appears often in nineteenth-century Florida. Natives of Trapani, Sicily, the Pacettis survived the New Smyrna ordeal and worked in St. Augustine, in the interior, and west coast of the state. In 1853, Andrew Pacetti reached Tampa, as a chainman of a surveying team. He remained, and in 1853, the citizens of Tampa elected him the first town marshal.

Captain A.N. Pacetti enlisted in the Third Seminole War, commanding a boat company scouring South Florida for the few Seminoles who remained. He carved into an ancient cypress tree, "Captain A.N. Pacetti, 10 September 1857." The inscription was found a century later!

The Leonardi/Leonardy family was also well known in early Florida. Rocco Leonardi left Modena to try his fortune at New Smyrna. He survived to marry Esperanza Valle. The *East Florida Papers* document that a Roque Leonardy requested permission from the governor of Florida to open a store and sell goods. In 1787, a Spanish census taker described Leonardi as "a farmer and storekeeper, owner of 4 houses, 2 horses, 1 slave, and 50 acres of land." He held the position of lieutenant of the city militia. Spanish officials bestowed the honorific title of "don" upon him. A number of his grandchildren left St. Augustine—by the Civil War, a struggling community—to try their fortune in Tampa.

Bartholemew, the son of Bartolome Leonardy and Antonia Bonelli, migrated to Tampa in 1845, played in Tampa's first brass band and also served on the City Council in the 1860s. The 1850 census listed two individuals residing at the Leonardy home: Adolphus Pesete, born in Florida in 1829, and a painter by trade, and Andrew Pallesseie, born in Florida in 1825 and a blacksmith. Most likely, Pallesseie was Andrew H. Pellicer, son of Martin and Magdalena Pacetti Pellicer of St. Augustine. His son was a leading druggist and manufacturer of Golden Eye Lotion and cough remedies. Vincent may have been the city's first architect, building several homes in the city. Captured by Union forces, he was imprisoned—ironically—at Fort Marion in St. Augustine. Released after the war, he moved to Tampa where he became a gentleman farmer and served on the City Council. The Leonardi grapefruit memorializes his legacy.

One of the most intriguing figures to fight in Florida was Colonel Louis W. Tinelli. A blue-blooded member of Italian royalty, he served in the Austro-Hungarian army in northern Italy, but lost his commission when his personal convictions for liberal reform became intertwined with his military duties. He was imprisoned in Piedmont jails for three years. When King Charles Albert became king in 1831, Tinelli was released from prison but banished. The romantic revolutionary immigrated to America, where his linguistic and diplomatic skills were appreciated by the US Department of State. When the Civil War erupted, Tonelli was a consul in Portugal. He soon returned and organized a volunteer unit to fight for the Union cause. A lieutenant colonel in the 90th New York Volunteer Infantry, he saw duty in Key West and the Dry Tortugas. He was one of the most prominent members of the famed Garibaldi Guard.

Italian-born Luigi Lomia settled in Texas, enlisted in the US Military Academy in 1863, and was assigned to a battery at Fort Brooke in 1880, shortly before the fort was decommissioned.

During the nineteenth century, Italy's greatest export was human capital. From the Alpine fields of the Piedmont to the wheat fields of

Catania, from the Po Valley to the hills of the Abruzzi, Italy hemor-rhaged people. But not all who left were peasants and artisans. The Roman Catholic Church also sent to the far corners of the world priests, nuns, and teachers to minister to the flocks.

Religious orders, such as the Scalabrinians, ministered to Italians far away from home. Another such order was the Congregation of the Holy Redeemer, a religious order founded in Scala, Italy, in 1732. In the fall of 1867, Bishop Augustin Verot, a devoted French cleric who dedi-cated his life to his calling in the Episcopal seat of St. Augustine, sum-moned four Redemptorists to Florida. The priests spent part of 1868 in Jacksonville and St. Augustine. In 1870, he recruited two priests from Genoa, Italy, to come to Key West. Father Felix Ghione studied at the seminary in Genoa, until Bishop Verot recruited him to minister the flock in Key West. Ghione spent nearly two decades in Key West, 1880–1898.

Tampa's anti-clerical climate invited Protestant missionaries to recruit wavering Catholics. In 1905, a Roman missionary named Evaristo Ghiodini arrived. He quickly erected a Methodist day school and his future work seemed bright until a tongue-wagging scandal chased him from the city. A journalist discovered that the man of God was living out of wedlock with an opera diva—who bore him two children! Ghiodini promptly left Tampa for Nashville, in the arms of another mistress!

The Italy of America

Following the Civil War, Florida, like other southern states, suffered economic woe and social dislocation. Under-populated, Florida's 1870 population was only 180,000, making it still, in the words of a New York journalist, "the smallest tadpole in the dirty pool of secession." For the next seventy years, Florida had the smallest population of any state in the South. Florida would not surpass the million resident plateau until 1920.

Florida was also isolated from the rest of the United States. Napoleon once suggested Italy was too long to be a nation; perhaps Florida is too long to be a single state. The distance from Key West to Pensacola equals that between Pensacola and Chicago.

Florida had one commodity to offer Americans and the world: land. Possessing 60,000 square miles of land, 600 miles of beach and 2,000 miles of coastline, Florida also boasts an extraordinary variety of landscape and ecosystems. To many nineteenth-century observers, Florida was "the Italy of America." This colorful phrase, scrolled beneath the banner of the *Fort Myers News-Press*, summoned readers and travelers. Europeans, too, conjured up romantic images of Florida. "What Italy is to Europe," proclaimed the *Edinburgh Courant* in 1883, "Florida is to the States of America, but in a much more prounced degree." The inspired publicist further insisted that Florida's climate rivaled that of Southern Italy; moreover, "nor can Naples boast of bluer skies than ours, or Florence of sweeter moonlight. . . ."

The Mediterranean provided countless travelers and writers a ready metaphor. To capitalize upon the association, boosters borrowed or corrupted Italian words to name and glamorize cities and places: Bari, Belleair, Florence Villa, Italia, Genoa, Limona, Naples, Venice, Salerno, Rialto, Vero Beach, and Zolfo Springs; Cafe Luna Rossa, Lido Key, the Rialto, Lake Como, Lugano, the Isle of Capri, Venetian Gardens, Venetian Isles, the Soreno Hotel, Villa Serena Apartments, the Belle Vista Lounge, the Hotel Florencia, the Gondola Bar, Capri Village, Il Cioppino, Café Limoncello, the Urbino Café, Rivoli Reserve, Venetian Hotel, Grande Bellagio Condominiums and Penthouses, Il Bellagio Restaurant, Roman Massages and Body Rubs, Tuscany Cove, Tuscany

Grill, Toscana Towers, Vivaldi, and many, many more. Dissonant names, such as Saraceno, sound better on a million-dollar condominium.

The state of Florida desperately wanted people to populate its vast space. In particular, they wished to replace freed African American slaves with the proper kind of white laborers. Developers, journalists, and promoters, however, were never of one mind whether Italians constituted the right type of "white" immigrant. On the one hand, Italians seemed perfectly suited for Florida's tropical climate. In particular, they brought centuries of experience tending citrus groves and could withstand the humid, mosquito-infested swamps and terrain. General Henry S. Sanford, formerly US Minister to Belgium and founder of the town on Lake Monroe bearing his name, declared that Italians represented "a most valuable class of immigrants . . . intelligent and industrious." In 1893, the famed journalist Amos Cummings visited General Sanford's estate. Writing for the *New York Sun,* Cummings observed,

> He [Sanford] has imported a colony of Swedes, who agree to work for him a specified time without wages, after which each one was to receive two acres for a homestead. Some of the destitute Italians who recently landed in New York have found their way to Sanford's grove, and are said to be doing good work.

Curiously, the author observed that many of the Swedes—the most desired of immigrant laborers—"had broken their contracts and deserted. . . ." Italians, too, soon departed.

Italiante influences shaped Gilded Age Florida. Italian artisans served as sculptors, painters, and gardeners on some of the grand buildings erected between 1870 and 1890. DeBary Hall, built by prominent wine merchant Samuel Frederick DeBary, was erected in 1871 in the city of DeBary, Volusia County. The architecture is elaborate.

The Florida and Southern press generally expressed a xenophobia and nativism all-too-familiar when the subject of Italian immigrants was debated. The *Gainesville Sun* opined that "the Italian is not trustworthy, honest nor a faithful kind of laborer . . . they are given to making trouble wherever they go." When the Jacksonville *Florida Times-Union* learned of an 1891 proposal to import Italian laborers, the paper asserted, "There should be no welcome for foreigners who are not willing to mingle and assimilate with the native element." In 1882, the *Tampa Sunday Tribune* observed, "Tampa was afflicted this weekend with a wheezy hand organ, run by an able-bodied Italian. He scooped up the dimes, however." The Florida Department of Agriculture, in a 1906 report, stated, "We do not want the people of Southern Europe, the Poles, the Hunns [*sic.*], and the Italians.. . . the classes of these people who emigrate are of the lowest order, . . . they are the breeders of socialism and anarchism." The *Wauchula Advocate* editorialized in 1911, "If Tampa would import a few hundred Irishmen with stout blackthorns it would have less trouble with its 'Eyetalians.'" In DeSoto County, the organizers of a new community unveiled a "Christian colony" in 1914. They specified: "No Negroes, No Dagoes." Writer and reformer Emily Fogg Meade, writing in *South Atlantic Quarterly* in 1905, cautioned, "The South should carefully consider this problem of immigration. . . . To the ordinary American, the Italian is a dirty, undersized individual who engages in degrading labor shunned by Americans and who is often a member of the Mafia." In 1901, the *Atlanta Journal* editorialized, "From Rome comes a report that 40,000 Italians are booked to leave for the U.S. during May. There is but one way to stop this flood of spaghetti emigration and that is to prohibit sidewalk fruit stands."

The late nineteenth century was a glorious time to be a European nobleman, even one without resources. The rising *nouveau riches* eagerly sought to marry their daughters to dukes and earls to legitimate their newly won status. One such match was the marriage of Nicole Tamajo, the Duke of Castellucia, and Jennie Anheuser, daughter of the German beer baron of St. Louis. In 1878, Tamajo purchased one of Florida's most famed orange groves, the Dummett Grove, located on Merritt Island in Brevard County. In 1881, he built "Dummett Castle," constructed of timber salvaged from the wreck, "Santa Cruz."

The 1880 and 1890 US Censuses offer tantalizing glimpses of Italians in Florida. In 1880, census takers counted 77 Italian natives, a figure that increased to 408 Italian immigrants a decade later. Curiously, Dade County—the future metropolis, listed no Italian residents. The largest "concentration" was in Escambia County, where Italians worked Pensacola's docks and fishing boats. The next largest number was in Marion County, where Italian vintners were attempting to establish a colony. In 1885, an immigration agent lured 200 Italian immigrants to the North-Central Florida settlement of Welshton (near Ocala). A Corsican-born priest, Dominique Andre Bottolaccio followed. The agricultural experiment failed, but many of the families (Toffaletti, Ghiotto, Guliano, and Pasetti) relocated to Palatka, Green Cove Springs, and Ocala.

The travails of Louis Toffaletti and Victoria Ghiotto Toffaletti marked a dark chapter of the immigration experience. In 1885, they left northern Italy to become landowners in Florida. The ship landed in Philadelphia, where a ship captain swindled them out of their funds. They managed to find their way to Green Cove Springs where a destitute colony struggled. In the early 1890s, several families moved to the Marion County community of Martí City, named for the Cuban patriot José Martí. Toffaletti became an elected official. The devastating freeze of 1895 and labor unrest doomed the cigar-making community, making it a ghost town. Most of the residents moved to Tampa.

Historians wishing to document the presence of migratory Italians are left with fragments of evidence. What is one to make of the two sentences of print appearing in the Tallahassee *Weekly Floridian*, 31 October 1891? "D.B. McKay of Tampa has 25 Italians to work on the new railroad from Bartow to Phosphoria. The ties and iron are all laid and only lining and surfacing remains to be done. . . ." What happened to the Italian laborers? Did they tell their children and grandchildren about working in such a strange and hostile place? Or did they remain contract laborers, never to marry? Or did the survivors, as old men, think of this episode as part of the price of the American Dream?

On May 14, 1892, Italian consul Ricardo Motta filed a report, "Emigrazione e Colonie." The Consul believed about 200 Italians lived in Pensacola, 30 in Key West, 80 in St. Cloud, and 250 in Tampa. The report's timing was significant. Two important events were occurring in 1892: the dissolution of a sugar colony in St. Cloud and the inception of Florida's most significant Italian colony in Tampa.

The St. Cloud experiment incorporated all of the elements in Italian immigrant history: dreams and desperation, serendipity and human agency. The Italian connection, seemingly insignificant, had enormous implications. In 1880, Philadelphia financier Hamilton Disston purchased four million acres of Central and South Florida property for a million dollars. Much of the land was under water. Disston envisioned a vast region populated by yeoman farmers. To finance his ambitious plans, Disston attempted the largest sugar plantation as yet conceived.

At this time, Louisiana was America's largest sugar producer. To cut the cane and process the juice, huge numbers of African Americans and Sicilians worked the southwest Louisiana parishes (including this author's grandparents, emigrants from Alia, who settled in Napoleonville). Work was intensely seasonal, so many laborers functioned as a floating proletariat, traveling far and wide, to the north on the Illinois Central, and east aboard steamships and freighters.

Around 1886, the first vanguard of Sicilian immigrants arrived in the Central Florida communities fancifully named St. Cloud and Runnymede (near Kissimmee). In April 1893, readers of the *New York Sun* read about the remarkable agriculture experiment occurring in Florida. New Yorkers surely must have stumbled upon the strange-sounding place names: Lakes Tahopekaliga, Istokpoga, and Hicpochee. "The Italians and negroes who work the fields have no use for a doctor," observed the *Sun* reporter." The first year they were taxed to support one, the same as under the Louisiana system. The second year they refused to pay for the tax. No one was sick, . . . there are many Italians (here) at work."

The survivors would have been amused *and* bemused to hear about the healing powers of plantation work. Work was brutal, but Sicilians did not come to America to spend their lives cutting sugar cane. Locals complained of Italian work habits and customs. "Italians as workmen do not shine," observed a St. Cloud resident in 1891. "The seven that worked for us today would individually or as a body take the cake anywhere for crass idiocy & laziness." Early in 1891, the *Kissimmee Leader* noted,

> A regular swarm of Dagos left Kissimmee Monday. After the gathering and grinding was finished at the sugar mill, the company instead of discharging the large gang of men they really did not need, reduced their wages. . . . The Dagos did not like this and so a big gang of them left for Ybor City.

The small contingent of Sicilians encountered a Spanish and Cuban enclave on the edge of Tampa. In 1891, Ybor City was a company town comprised of one thousand highly skilled, Spanish-speaking cigar makers. The Spaniards and Cubans welcomed the Sicilians who saw a future in the fledgling community. By May 1892 the Italian consul observed, "The [Italian] colony in general is prosperous but does not own property or land." The infamous "Mafia" riot in 1891 New Orleans brought more Sicilians to Tampa.

Privation and sacrifice characterized the early years of Ybor City. The industrial community had literally been carved out of a wilderness; wolves and alligators became neighbors and predators. "What I saw before me almost brought me to tears," remembered Giovanni Cacciatore, and early pioneer who had worked in St. Cloud and Ybor City. He had been interviewed by WPA workers in the 1930s. "There was nothing," he said, recalling early Ybor City. "When his wife arrived, she burst into tears. 'Why have you brought me to such a place?'" Paolo Longo arrived in Ybor City around the turn of the century. He told this interviewer seventy-five years later, when asked his impression of Tampa: "Zanzare e cocodrilli!" [mosquitoes and alligators!].

Immigration is destiny. And sometimes immigrants are victims of destiny. The decades spanning the late nineteenth century unleashed revolutions in technology and communications. Bridging Florida was a daunting challenge. It is a state of vast distances. Italians helped build narrow gauge railroads as well as Henry Flagler's monuments to cross the Florida Keys by bridge and rail.

In 1886, the Russian-born aristocrat and lumberman Peter Demens obtained a charter to build the Orange Belt Railway between Longwood and St. Petersburg. Many Italians worked on that line. W.H. Reams, when recalling his 1880s boyhood in Winter Park, remembered "Italian laborers with their wheelbarrows and shovels making the grade." Italian laborers nearly rioted during the summer of 1887, threatening to lynch Demens unless they were paid.

Immigrants, desperate to earn money, performed myriad tasks. Decades later, their children and grandchildren must have marveled at their pluck and occasional luck. Gaetano Ferlita, a survivor of the St. Cloud experience, helped build the magnificent Tampa Bay Hotel.

Constructed in the late 1880s, the hotel still stands, today as the University of Tampa. Several Sicilian tinsmiths worked on the thirteen minarets that graced the hotel.

Corporations sought out-of-state and foreign labor to construct these massive projects. One source of labor was the Italian *padrone* system [contract labor]. *Padroni* recruited laborers based typically upon the workers' nationality and skills. The bosses frequently charged the laborers as well as the contractors a fee based on the days worked and the number of recruits. The exploitation included incidental charges, such as inflated costs of transportation, lodging, food, and insurance. Numerous protests were filed by Italian consuls and reformers about the miserable conditions. Workers struck, but generally they were powerless. In 1906, fifty Italian immigrants worked at a lumber camp near Lake City in North Florida. In 1907, Count Marconi came to Florida to investigate charges of peonage on the East Coast Railroad. Apologists argue that the *padrone* was a necessary evil. Italians needed *padroni* such as V. Palumbo; otherwise, many might not have had any jobs.

V. Palumbo was a New York Italian labor boss who recruited workers for Henry Flagler's Florida East Coast Railroad. In the late 1890s and early 1900s, he supplied hundreds of workers to the Florida East Coast Railroad for wages of $1.25 a day. In a February 1902 letter in *L'Araldo Italiano* [The Italian Herald], a New York City newspaper, Palumbo wrote:

> The workers that I sent to Florida arrived in a healthy place, where there is absolutely no malaria. . . . I have been in negotiations . . . to establish an agricultural colony in the vicinity of St. Augustine and Miami. The land is adaptable to the cultivation of vines and fruits, and the climate is identical to Sicily. . . . I have found a terrestrial paradise. . . . Then to Florida!

The history of Italians who fell the trees, leveled the grade, and picked the crops is largely forgotten. These were men on the move, so census takers rarely documented their presence. Their legacy endures in the things they built and tales told at family reunions.

When the nineteenth century dawned, the future of Italians in Florida was uncertain. A handful of Italians had survived the ignominy of New Smyrna and resided in St. Augustine. If asked, they would not likely have identified themselves as Italian. They were a minority in a Spanish and Minorcan city; moreover, their very presence was as precarious as was Spain's tenuous hold upon *La Florida.*

A century later, small clusters of Italians could be found in colonies, work camps, and homes from Pensacola to Key West. Their legacies can be found in the heart of pine forests they felled, the prodigious quantities of fish caught, the sugar cane they cut, and the cigars they rolled.

Italian signatures exist, most eloquently and fittingly in St. Augustine. In the mid-1880s, the Robber Baron Henry Flagler selected the Ancient City as the spot he would invest his vast fortune. In 1888, the lavish Ponce de Leon Hotel opened, soon followed by the magisterial Alcazar and Cordova Hotels. Scores of Italian artists, sculptors, and craftsmen left their imprint on these monuments. The Italian artist Virgilio Tojetti (1849–1901) painted murals of cupids and angels in the grand parlor. The hotel sold post cards of Tojetti's paintings, souvenirs that can be purchased on eBay today.

When Flagler's beloved daughter died in 1889, he dedicated St. Augustine's magnificent Memorial Presbyterian Church in her name. Built in a Venetian Renaissance style, the stunning structure featured a copper-clad Venetian dome, Italian marble tile, and a Siennese-carved marble baptismal font.

Constructed of the finest New and Old World materials and artisans, the Flagler Memorial Church and the Ponce de Leon Hotel will endure for centuries. Less permanent and more fleeting are the memories of Italian immigrants who labored long hours for preciously little. The immigrant peddler personified the sacrifices of the first generation. Italians peddled fruits and vegetables, sharpened knives and scissors, and hawked fish and fowl on crude carts and mule-powered wagons.

The press maintained an uneasy relationship with the Italian peddler. In 1897, the *Tampa Morning Tribune* admitted that the "Goo Goos" [good government types] had indeed cleaned up streets by restricting peddling, but confessed to a "monumental dullness after dark." In their absence, "Italian fruit dealers" brought cheer and color to the streets, "often in front of a roasting fire of peanuts."

In 1915, the Tampa City Council banned "dancing monkeys" and "hand organs." The *Morning Tribune* editorialized, "The hand-organ man and his monkey are one of the institutions of a happy childhood. What man of us who does not remember with the quickening pulses of youth the days we followed the Sicilian itinerant and his capering simian from block to block innocently gleeful as we watched its inimitable reception of the tossed coin and the donated peanut?"

A City Called Ybor

For all of the ballyhoo and promotion, few Italian immigrants became rural dwellers. For most immigrants, Florida was simply too distant, too rural, and too risky to leave New York City or Chicago. Florida, however, boasted one remarkable Italian colony that not only survived but thrived: Ybor City.

What might have been a temporary refuge became a permanent colony. Each week in the 1890s, more Italians chose to cast their fortunes in this distant town with the strange name: Ybor City. In March 1899, the local paper confirmed what residents already knew: the emergence of a "Little Italy." What strangers saw as a mass of undifferentiated Italians was in reality a tight-knit cluster of Sicilians from a small number of towns on the southwestern island: Santo Stefano di Quisquina, Alessandria della Rocca, and Contessa Entellina. The community of Contessa Entellina is especially interesting because its residents were Albanese, descendents of Albanians who had fled the Turks centuries earlier. Contessiotti spoke with a distinctive dialect, called "Geg Geg." The decade of the 1890's saw Tampa's Italian population grow from 56 to 1,315. By 1910 the population doubled.

Italians quickly realized the importance of group solidarity. In an 1896 newspaper report, an article mentioned that widespread suffering existed among the immigrant groups in Ybor City. Quickly a group of Italians signed a letter stating that they had "failed to discover a single case of distress among the resident Italian colony." In 1894 a group had bound together to create Florida's first Italian mutual aid society. Thus began La Societá Italiana di Mutuo Soccorso or l'Unione Italiana (the Italian Union or Club).

By 1900 Tampa's Little Italy had evolved to include significant numbers of women and children. Sicilian women played an indispensable role in the community. Women found ample employment in the burgeoning cigar industries; indeed, Italian women soon surpassed the number of Italian men in the factories. A curious pattern emerged as women became the steady wage earners while men began dairies or started grocery stores. Italian women generally began their work careers in the lowest paying jobs—as "strippers"—literally stripping or taking the stem from the tobacco leaf. They quickly advanced to higher paying positions. By the 1920s, Italian immigrant women equaled the numbers of immigrant men—a rarity in American history.

Making Havana Cigars at the factory of SANCHEZ & HAYA COMPANY, makers of the Finest Havana Cigars, Factory No. 1, Tampa, Florida.

Cigarmakers at the Ybor City factory of Sanchez & Haya Company in about 1910. University of South Florida Special Collections.

Italians quickly established a distinctive identity. The local press was especially intrigued by a special Italian culture of death. In October 1893, the local Tampa paper described an Italian funeral, with a "corpse carried by four large men with uplifted hats, followed by a brass band, then an empty hearse and carriage preceding the regular concourse of sorrowing relatives and sobbing friends." By 1900, an Italian cemetery had materialized. In short time, the brass bands died out, but not the cemetery, which still exists.

Often customs must have struck Americans as very odd. In 1914, the *Tampa Daily Times* reported an incident involving several young Italian boys who accidentally hit an elderly Sicilian woman. The dispute was settled when the boys were forced to kiss the feet of the woman.

Italian immigrants had entered a Florida community of radical ideas and labor conflict. Angelo Massari, an impoverished Sicilian emigrant, wrote in his autobiography, "When in 1902 I landed in Tampa, I found myself in a world of radicals for which I was prepared. In Tampa, anarchism and socialism flourished." Ironically, Massari became a successful international banker!

Women often formed the rank and file in the unfolding labor conflicts. In November 1910, a *Tampa Tribune* reporter left this account of a strike:

> At the factory of Arguelles, Lopez and Bros., nine Italian women gave an entertainment. . . . The misguided ones, armed with clubs paraded the streets about the factory. Their weapons they brandished and their tongues they did wag, giving vent to threats that they would beat to death all who would work.

The most notorious event involving Italians in modern Florida occurred in 1910. In Tampa, immigrant cigarmakers struck once again that year. This was no ordinary labor disturbance; rather, it was a general strike involving 12,000 employees. In August 1910, a *Tampa Tribune* reporter described a crowd that included "bevies of gaily dressed Spanish, Cuban, and Italian women," all waving red bandanas.

In September 1910, shots were fired from a crowd of Italian and Cuban strikers gathered outside the Bustillo & Díaz Factory. One of the bullets struck and killed an American bookkeeper. Authorities quickly arrested two Italian immigrants, Angelo Albano and Castenge (Costanzo) Ficarotta. The press indicted the two suspects, branding them "tools of anarchistic elements in this city."

In what amounted to a conspiracy, Tampa police decided to move Albano and Ficarotta to a West Tampa jail. On the corner of Grand Central (today's Kennedy Blvd) and Howard Avenue, an angry mob awaited the prisoners. Police turned the men over to the vigilantes who hanged them. Perpetrators pinned a note to Albano: "Beware! . . . We know seven more. We are watching you." Quickly, post cards celebrated the hanging. Governor Albert Gilchrist banned the sale of such post cards, not because of the graphic images, but because negative publicity might hurt tourism. The hanging endures as the worst mass lynching in the history of Tampa.

In 2001, conductor and impresario Anton Coppola chose Tampa as the world's premier for his opera, *Sacco and Vanzetti*. Few Tampans

were alive to appreciate the historical jus-
tice of the maestro's decision. In August
1927, 15,000 cigarmakers walked out of
factories to protest the plight of the Italian
anarchists. The Italian Club served as a
shelter, forum, and cathedral during the
trial and execution.

What is most striking about the Italians
in Ybor City was their interaction with their
neighbors. While Cubans (Black and White),
Spaniards, and Italians each had their rec-
ognizable, self-contained Little Havana,
Little Italy, and mutual aid societies, Ybor
City was a remarkably diverse and fluid
place; indeed, the working-class neighbor-

USF Library,
Special Collections.

hoods may have been the South's most tolerant areas. Black Cubans
lived and worked by the side of "white" immigrants. To be sure, when
Americans wished to ridicule Italians, they called them "Cuban niggers,"
but within the sheltered enclave, Italians found comfort and solidarity.

The most significant transformation in Ybor City occurred in the
1920s. Italians, Cubans, and Spaniards became, in the local vernacular,
"Latins." While each group possessed strong ethnic identities (and
resistance lingered over ethnic intermarriage), first and second generations became Latins. The term Hispanic was never used in Tampa until
the 1970s.

Several factors explain the new Latin identity. First, Tampa's
"Anglo" population never fully accepted a Catholic immigrant workforce
(ironically, Latins in Ybor City were notoriously anti-clerical). This writer
interviewed many elderly Italians in the 1970s, who still bristled over
nativist hostilities. In general, Tampans tended to regard Ybor City as an
exotic, romantic place, until labor unrest erupted. "The European group
of humanity has a volcanic tendency that is well nigh universal," railed
the *Tampa Tribune*. Americans also protested and objected to the Latin's
proclivities toward celebration and their virulent anti-clericalism.

Ybor City's ferocious labor unrest united Italians, Cubans, and
Spaniards. More than anything else, the protracted labor strikes and

the messages emanating from the leftist press and tribune preached a need for solidarity. *El Lector* [The Reader] played a pivotal role in the labor movement and neighborhood. Latins hired a person to read to them while they made cigars. The reader always read in Spanish, and since Spanish was the community's lingua franca, by 1920, nearly all Italians spoke Spanish. Several Italians, such as Calogero Palermo, became readers. Since cigarmakers dictated what books would be read, workers acquired a classical education. Authors such as Victor Hugo preached solidarity and brotherhood. A vigorous and voluminous Spanish/Italian-language press complemented the readers. Italian newspapers included *L'Aurora, La Voce della Colonia, L'Orga-nizzatore, Il Martire,* and *The Florida Italian Bulletin.*

By the 1920s, a sense of permanence characterized Ybor City's Little Italy. Most notably, Italians expressed awe and pride in the construction (1918) of the four-story, neo-classical L'Unione Italiana. The Italian Club still stands today as one of the most picturesque and impressive monuments to Italian Americans. Marble, cast-iron balustrades, and a tiled cantina reflect pride and old-world craftsmanship.

The clubhouse of L'Unione Italiana, or Italian Club, was built at a cost of $80,000 in 1917, and it is still in operation in Ybor City. Tampa-Hillsborough County Library System.

The Italian Club was not simply a beautiful building. Immigrants and their children invested their energies and talents into the sanctuary, what one person called "a cathedral for the working classes." The club offered Italians a vibrant social life: dances on Saturday night, picn i c s on Sunday, Tito Schipa, Marie D'Amore, and Enrico Caruso singing opera on special occasions. In 1912, a newspaper headline announced, "Italians Plan Big Spectacle: Will Show Fall of Herculaneum." The spectacle required a cast of hundred. The club also functioned as a safety net. Members received progressive medical care; an adjacent building served as a medical clinic. Members received reduced prescriptions and a free burial plot in the Italian Club cemetery (and, until 1918, a brass band to accompany the cortege).

Ybor City has become a cottage industry, with a dozen books covering subjects from Afro-Cubans to cigar factories to mutual aid societies. A number of memoirs have also contributed to our understanding of this special place. Not all reflections depict Ybor City in warm and nostalgic terms. One of the most penetrating is *A Stranger in the Barrio* (2004) by Frank Urso. Urso's Ybor City was contested terrain. Growing up in the late 1930s and 1940s, Urso remembered his Sicilian parents laboring in the sweaty cigar factories for meager wages, the victims of a cruel economy and Cuban and Spanish bosses. African Americans who poured into the Latin neighborhood threatened Urso personally and Ybor City generally. After a successful medical career, Urso retired to Naples, Florida, where he passed away in 2008.

A Count's Tour of Florida

Jacksonville was Florida's largest city, but was never a magnet for large numbers of Southern and Eastern European immigrants. The 1890 census listed 46 Italians residing in Duval County, a figure that increased to only 149 by 1910. In 1911, Count G. Moroni toured the South, reporting that Jacksonville's Italian population was approximately 200. Italians toiled as farm laborers, tailors, fruit dealers, peanut peddlers, masons, and barbers. Six Italians worked on the railroad. J.A. Bianco & Brother advertised "fashionable tailors," while Carmini Castellano operated a fruit market and was the head of Florida Macaroni Works. Pantaleo Giupponi began work as a tailor but by 1926 owned a well-known delicatessen. Corrado's Italian Band was a fixture at concerts at Phoenix Park. Moroni's report may be found in *Bolletino dell'Emigrazione,* a valuable resource.

In St. Augustine, once the center of the country's earliest Italian population, Count Moroni found only five Italians. In the future metropolis of Miami, he encountered only 15 Italians and a few more in Key West, who were engaged in fishing and cigar manufacturing. "Pensacola's Italian colony consists of about 200 persons," he observed, "some employed in small shops, others engaged in barbering, shoe repair, and fishing. . . . In Apalachicola, one finds a few Italian fishermen, including some engaged in the oyster trade." The consul also discovered several hundred Italian phosphate miners in Polk County and railroad workers. He was appalled at the miners' living conditions, five to six immigrants sharing a small sleeping room, wages of $1 to $1.50 a day, "con un boss Americano."

Horatio Algers

In the early decades of the twentieth century, a photographer came to Florida. Such visitations were commonplace, since the Sunshine State trafficked in lush and exotic locales. But Lewis Hine was not interested in beach dunes or bird rookeries. Hine was bent upon exposing child labor, and nothing drove his message with more poignancy than a black and white photograph.

Between 1906 and 1913, Hine brought his camera and glass negatives to Tampa, Jacksonville, and Apalachicola. In Tampa, Hine found ample evidence of child labor. Sicilian immigrants survived the harsh conditions of urban America, in part, through a family economy that utilized children's earnings. Many Sicilians in Tampa recalled the use of *carusi,* children employed in the sulphur mines of Cianciana. In 1980, ex-cigar maker Louis Spoto told this author, "I never saw a paycheck until I got married." Similarly, Joe Maniscalco recalled, "I used to shine shoes as a kid. I used to go down to the old county courthouse around 5:30 in the morning and come back at midnight."

The Lewis Hine photographs attracted the attention of New Englander Joe Manning, who has embarked upon a lifelong quest to identify the anonymous children. One photograph is especially arresting. A barefooted young boy, a festering sore on his left leg, his left arm clutching a newspaper almost big as he, gazes at the photogra-

Young Cigarmakers in Englahardt & Co., Tampa, FL. There boys looked under 14. Work was slack and youngsters were not being employed much. Labor told me in busy times many small boys and girls are employed. Youngsters all smoke. Witness Sara R. Hine. Location: Tampa, Florida. Hine, Lewis Wickes, 1874–1940, photographer.

pher. The *scugnizzo* [street urchin] seems better placed in Naples than Tampa. A trash bin frames the photo. The cherubic face, however, belongs on a Caravaggio canvass. What happened to the lad? Did he become a beggar or a thief?

We now know the identity of the young boy. The 1913 photograph depicted six-year-old Gaetano "Tony" Valenti, the son of Sicilian immigrant Giuseppe Valenti. Giuseppe died of a ruptured appendix, forcing his young sons, Tony and J.C., to work. All six Valenti sons followed their father into the produce business. Tony, the penniless newsboy, achieved the American Dream: in his 68 years he founded a successful company, married Mary Scolaro,

One of America's youngest newsboys. 4 years old and regular seller; in Tampa, FL. Hine, Lewis Wickes, 1874- 1940, photographer.

raised three children, and was a pillar in the community. And he sold newspapers!

Ybor City was only the most spectacular manifestation of Italians in Florida between the 1890s and 1920s. Historians discount the validity of the Horatio Alger "rags-to-riches" model, but a few Italians did achieve impressive successes. Santa Rosa County in northwest Florida seemed like an unlikely place to find Italian success stories; if immigrants were found at all, they most likely would have been wielding an axe or saw. Santa Rosa County was fabulously rich in yellow pine and swamp cypress, raw materials America needed for expansion. Italians played an important role in the lumber industry. The Piaggio, Parodi, and Rosasco families owned and operated lumber camps and mills at Bay Point, sending a great deal of yellow pine and live oak timber to Italian ports on boats their consortium controlled. Between 1897 and 1904, the Rosascos bought out the Parodi interests. The sale was consummated at the US consulate offices in Genoa, Italy. For years, mill hands and bosses used the term "Genoa Pine" as a special grade of lumber. His vast operations included the Bagdad Sash Door and Blind factory, which burned to the ground in 1903.

The Rosasco family originated from Genoa, Italy, settling first in California. This was no ordinary immigrant family. William S. Rosasco was born in Oakland, California, and educated in England. His bride was a graduate of the Conservatory of Bologna. The family made a fortune in the tugboat and shipping business before moving to Florida in 1885, where they opened the Santa Rosa Lumber Company. For over a century, the Rosascos have played a prominent role in the mercantile and banking interests of Northwest Florida. They also became involved in the social and civic affairs of the area. During World War II, William S. Roscasco, a native of Pensacola and graduate of the University of Pennsylvania, was chairman of Pensacola chapter of the American Red Cross.

The April 2006 obituary of Angela Rosasco can only begin to touch a life that spanned 109 years and three centuries. Born in Viguzzolo in Northwest Italy, she came to America in 1915. She worked as a model and fashion designer in New York City until 1970.

Adelia Rosasco-Soule has left a touching and invaluable account of her family's life in Northwest Florida, entitled *Panhandle Memories*

(1987). Born in 1901, Adelia recalled the lives of her cultured Italian family in a hardscrabble section of Florida that they came to revere. "I was Mamma's 'Italian child,'" she wrote. "Bringing up a catholic family 'in the woods' was not an easy task for a cultivated Italian woman," she remembered. "Mass was said once a month in our parlor." Adelia described her Aunt Mariah:

> To birth, breast feed, and raise a brood of children at a sawmill town in the piney woods, five miles from a doctor was no easy job. . . . She's be making shirts for the boys . . . and she'd tell me how lonesome it was to have no church, no sisters or brothers or Eyetalian family. . . .

Adelia Rosasco-Soule was honored as the poet laureate of West Florida. She died in 1996.

The most notable Italian businessman in late nineteenth- and early twentieth-century Florida was the redoubtable Peter Tomasello Sr. Born in Trieste in 1861, he served in the Austro-Hungarian army as a bodyguard to Emperor Franz Josef. Wounded at Sarajevo in 1880, he recovered and immigrated to America. He landed in Pensacola in October 1881 during a yellow fever epidemic.

Tomasello took a job as a sawyer at Bay Point. Within fifteen years he had married, established a homestead in the mill town of Bagdad, and become principal owner in the Bay Point and Robinson Point plants. His lumber operations expanded greatly, as did his political and social involvement in the community. He also operated Tomasello's Bath House at Oakland Basin. Chairing the Santa Rosa Board of County Commissioners, during World War I he served on the US Shipping Board as a "dollar-a-year-man." A son Giovanni enlisted in the US Army and was killed in a poison gas attack. Another son Dewey was gassed at the Second Battle of the Marne but survived. Still another son became a prominent Florida politician. In 1923 the elder Tomasello moved to Osceola County in Central Florida where he built several new lumber mills. When he died in 1938, the Jacksonville *Florida Times Union* eulogized that Peter Tomasello "was recognized throughout the State as a one of its leaders in the lumber and sawmill business of West Florida when that section was a wild and virgin territory."

Fishermen

Every Florida seaport attracted Italian fisherman, sailors, and stevedores. In Pensacola, "the Red Snapper capital of the world," scores of Italians sailed to the snapper banks of the Gulf of Mexico to fetch the prized catch. By 1915, Pensacola had a foreign-born population of one thousand, of which several hundred were Italian. The censuses document Italian names such as Batta, Cafiero, DiFusco, Mirabella, and Strazzola. The Little Italy section of Pensacola was located between Barcelona and Coyle, Garden and Main streets.

Apalachicola, Pensacola, Panama City, Cedar Key, Tampa, and Key West included Italians in the ranks of pioneering fishermen. Jimmy Nichols, a four-time mayor of Apalachicola, recalled in an 1989 interview his memories of Franklin County between 1900 and 1930:

> Been in Apalachicola all my life. . . . When I was a young teenager, downtown Water Street and Commerce Street were full of Italians and Greeks. They were doing their fishing and oystering; they even had some sponging going on. (When) you walked down the streets, you couldn't hear English spoken. It was either Greek or Italian. Down here, around where the courthouse is located now, there were Italian bakers makin' these round rolls of bread—those Italians would open it up and put olive oil and pepper on it.

Joseph Messina's oyster cannery, Apalachicola, 1920.
Florida State Archives.

Genaro "Jiggs" Zingarelli exemplifies the Italian contribution to Apalachicola. His grandfather came from Puglia, and the family eventually settled in Franklin County, Florida. Born in 1915, "Jiggs" attended local schools, served in WWII, and returned to take a job as a printer. In addtion, he also specialized in making oyster tags (an industry requirement) the old-fashioned way (by hand).

Anthony Taranto's Italian-born parents met in Apalachicola. In 1923, they opened Taranto's Seafood. Anthony, born in 1932, ran the family business until it closed in the late 1990s.

Oyster shuckers in Apalachicola, Fla. This work is carried on by many young boys during busy seasons. This is a dull year so only a few youngsters were in evidence. Location: Apalachicola, Florida.
Hine, Lewis Wickes, 1874–1940, photographer.

In addition to fishing, Italians filled the niches in Northwest Florida communities. In Panama City, Ralph Sorrentino worked as a barber. But the enterprising immigrant also organized a band that played for special occasions. He also offered music lessons from his home. Frank Pericola, the son of Italian immigrants who settled in Mississippi, worked as a journalist for the *Pensaolca Journal* and *Panama City News Herald.* He died in 1982. Alex Ceruti was a master carpenter and boat builder in Panama City.

The most dramatic evidence of the Italian contribution to the southern fishing industry occurred on the Florida-Georgia coastal border. The

St. Marys River straddles the states of Florida and Georgia, and the off-shore and tidal waters offered early settlers bountiful harvests. Local fishermen moved frequently between the two states and the communities of St. Marys, Thunderbolt, Fernandina, and Amelia Island.

In Thunderbolt, Georgia, Paul Cannella and the Maggioni family played instrumental roles. Cannella pioneered commercial shrimping and by the 1920s, Thunderbolt alone was harvesting and processing five million pounds of shrimp annually. L.P. Maggioni & Company was one of the first establishments to can prawns and shellfish. In addition, the Aiotta, Cafiero, Cesoroni, DeGracia, and Ricupero families also fished the local waters. Over 100 shrimp trawlers sailed from Thunderbolt harbor in the 1930s and 1940s. Most of the trawlers plied the waters between May and January, and fished the waters between Charleston, South Carolina, and St. Augustine, Florida. The industry peaked in the 1970s, and today exists barely as a reminder of its former glory.

The Maggioni family left the province of Treviglio in Italy. Young Lewis Paul became a cabin boy, eventually settling along the Gulf coast. His son Gilbert Philip became a major fish and shrimp wholesaler, with fleets and stores in Georgia, but also St. Augustine and Fernandina, Florida. His was the first company to can shrimp in glass jars. By 1950s, G.P. Maggioni had 2,500 employees and a national reputation. Each Palm Sunday, the bishop presided over the Blessing of the Fleets.

Paul and Vincent Cannerella, the sons of a Sicilian emigrant who had first settled in New York, eventually moved to Fernandina, Florida, the birthplace of modern shrimping. The Cannerellas were the first to popularize shrimp boiled at the docks and carried away by customers.

Fernandina, Florida, boasts that it is the "birthplace of modern shrimping." One of the oldest settlements in Florida, Fernandina and its fine harbor attracted a diverse population to its docks, wharves, and businesses. The exporting of lumber and phosphate, along with fishing, constituted the city's economy. Until the late nineteenth century, shrimping was a minor sideline in the larger harvest of mullet, red snapper, pompano, and other market fishes.

The arrival of Michele "Mike" Salvador (Salvatore) changed the industry's course. A Sicilian emigrant, he and his family had fished for generations. He quickly seized upon the possibilities of shrimping.

Salvador and his Sicilian brothers-in-law Antonio Poli and Salvatore Versaggi pioneered a number of techniques that revolutionized the harvest of shrimp: the use of mechanization to catch, process, and distribute the product. They later perfected the use of the otter trawl, which greatly increased their yields. By 1917, Fernandina was harvesting 10 million pounds of shrimp.

In Florida, Italian fishermen commanded important positions as wholesalers, captains, and crewmen. In a 1902 report, the Italian consul listed 200 Italian fishermen in Pensacola. The individual stories are compelling. At age ten, Giovanni Savarese left Naples to join his brother Luigi in Savannah, Georgia. Giovanni migrated to Tampa in 1885, lured in part, by the opening of Henry Plant's Railroad. Refrigerated cars could now whisk Gulf of Mexico pompano and green turtles to New York's Fulton Street markets. By the 1890s, the Savarese fleet boasted hundreds of fishing vessels, including one large steam boat. "Savarese & Co. are making the scales fly in the fish trade," applauded the *Tampa Tribune* in 1901. King Victor Emmanuel III decorated Savarese with the Cross of a Cavalier of the Crown of Italy. Illustrative of the ability of successful Italians to integrate into "Anglo" society, John Savarese founded and served as commodore of the Tampa Yacht and Country Club.

The Massalina family is legendary in Panama City and Bay County. Massalina Bayou honors the family's contribution. In 1875, the Massalinas moved to Redfish Point in Bay County, where they fished and built sailboats. Narcisco Massalina, nicknamed "Hawk," lived more than a century, dying in 1948 at the age of 108. In 1941, Massalina's shipyards were seized by the US government to create a military base, Tyndall Field.

The Mediterranean of America

To cook *scungilli alle limone* [conch with lemon] and *pasta con carciofi* [spaghetti with artichokes], hundreds of Italian chefs came to Florida during the great land boom of the 1920s. Cities that did not exist or were mere villages in 1900 burst like the proverbial pomegranate. In the 1920s, Florida became deeply ingrained in the American consciousness. Florida's attributes and values—hype, promotion, and sensuality—appealed to the fast-paced lifestyle of the Roaring Twenties. Miami, Miami Beach, Coral Gables, Palm Beach, and Boca Raton became some of the most seductive addresses in the United States. An Italian chef and marble sculptor seemed at home in such lush surroundings.

Architecture has been described as "frozen music." An architectural style matched developers' dreams to make Florida into an American Mediterranean. The press called the style Mediterranean Revival, an eclectic blend of Italian, Spanish, and Moorish elements into a look that seemed to fit: stucco walls, intense pastel colors, serpentine columns, terra cotta roof tiles, patios with fountains and statuary, and blazing hibiscus and bougainvillea.

The 1920s and 1930s profoundly altered the rhythms of Italian

One of Temple Terrace's many Mediterranean Revivals, located on Glen Arven Drive, 1925

America. Most dramatically, the Immigration Restriction Acts cut off the source of Italians; henceforth, the colony, neighborhood, and schools would be the critical agents of change. Large numbers of children guaranteed energy and dynamism for the next generation. Prohibition, enacted in 1920 and lasting through 1933, also supplied new opportunities. Since Florida's spacious coastline permitted easy entry of boats laden with Cuban rum and Bahaman-British gin, enterprising individuals willing to take chances could and did earn quick money.

Florida became Florida in the 1920s, a state identified with dreams and a place of dreamscapes. The image of the Sunshine State as a Mediterranean escape was popularized in endless promotions. Nowhere was the boom louder than in the Southeast. In Coral Gables, Boca Raton, and Palm Beach, architects unveiled a style that borrowed heavily from Italy, Spain, North Africa, and Greece. Called Med-Rev, Mediterranean Revival was an American invention. To make brand-new homes resemble seaside villas that had stood for centuries on Málaga or Portofino, contractors borrowed liberally from Renaissance Europe and the California Mission styles, plus American ingenuity. Alexander P. Moore, once ambassador to Spain, is said to have gasped upon first seeing Addison Mizner's Palm Beach, "It's more Spanish than anything I ever saw in Spain!" Patios were called *piazzas*; balconies became *mezzanines*; poured cement reappeared as *terrazzo*. American *prominenti* demanded authenticity, so large numbers of Italian artisans—*muratore, scultore, e giardiniere*—were imported. The Italian words *loggia, cupola,* and *piazza* appeared in real estate advertisements, adding an aura of romance to a mundane home.

If "Italy-in-America" had a formal beginning in Florida, the epiphany occurred on the shorline of Key Biscayne in 1913–14 Miami. Charles Deering, a fabulously wealthy industrialist, wished to recreate a palace he had so admired in his visits to Italy and Spain. A millionaire with a keen palate and refined taste, Deering hired leading architecht Paul Chalfin to bring about the audacious project.

Deering christened his 40-room, 180-acre fantasy Villa Vizcaya. Completed in 1916, Vizcaya—named after a province in Spanish Basque—drew its inspiration from the Baroque era, especially Venetian art and building.

Vizcaya borrowed literally and figuratively from Italy and Venice. Venetian doges who had plundered jewels and holy relics for the glory of Christendom and Greater Venice would have appreciated Deering's purchases. The reception room was decorated with Venetian mirrors and items taken from the Palazzo Rossi in Venice. Ferrara furnished trunks of sixteenth-century tapestries destined for Miami. The east loggia's eighteenth-century cedar doors and sculpted decorations came from the Palazzo Torlonia in Rome. The ceiling in the music room was a reproduction of the sixteenth-century Palazzo Gonzaga in Mantua. The tearoom was distinctively Neapolitan. The famous marble fountain in the garden was designed by sixteenth-century architect Giacomo Barozzi di Vignola.

Addison Mizner, who reinvented Palm Beach and invented Boca Raton (Spanish for mouth of a rat!), was a man of exquisite tastes and bohemian habits. He was also architect and developer whose works dazzle admirers nearly a century later. In Palm Beach, he designed and

*"Playa Riente," residence of Joshua S. Cosden and later of Mrs. Hugh Dillman, view from the garden. Palm Beach. Credit: from **Florida Architecture of Addison Mizner,** 1928.*

built Playa Rienta in 1923. Italian artisans painted frescoes and constructed a loggia to resemble the Davanzati Palace in Florence.

In 1926, when architects rebuilt the Breakers, Henry Flagler's magnificent hotel in Palm Beach, they modeled the structure after the sixteenth-century Villa Medici. Appropriately, Italian craftsmen were imported to construct and decorate the opulent hotel.

Italian names glamorized 1920's Florida. Architect Frank Wyatt Woods built a number of homes in Coral Gables' Italian Village. The founder of Coral Gables, the visionary George Merrick, filled a limestone quarry with artesian water and christened the complex the Venetian Pool. In Winter Park, Bear Island was renamed the Isle of Sicily. Carl Fisher, the larger-than-life developer of Miami Beach, imported genuine Italian gondoliers to reinforce the Magic City's image as the American Venice.

When New York City Mayor Jimmy Walker asked John D. Ringling why he built his art museum in Sarasota rather than the Big Apple, the latter responded, "Because I don't like New York and I do like Sarasota!" The circus magnate fell in love with the city of the dulcet name astride the Gulf of Mexico. A bigger than life character, he was the master of "the greatest show on earth," the Ringling Circus. He and his wife Mabel had spent long periods of time in Italy. His monuments

Sarasota County; Sarasota Tourism.

matched his lofty ambitions, none more grandiose than his dream home. Called Ca' d'Zan (Venetian for the House of John), Ringling's mansion resembled a Doge's palace on the Grand Canal. The building was modeled after Venice's Ca' d'Oro. An authentic Venetian gondola sat on the dock. Surrounding his palace was a 68-acre bayfront estate. The centerpiece was his art gallery, built to house his incomparable collection. Ringling imported cargoes of Baroque masterpieces, with a special fondness for Italian masters: Tintoretto, Titian, Tiepolo,

Granacci, Filippo Lippi, Luca Della Robbia, Raphael, Uccello and Il
Guercino. Literally and figuratively, Ringling borrowed heavily from
Italian Renaissance villas. Eleventh-century marble columns and inlaid
Florentine doorways decorate the loggia. Brightly-colored, glazed
terra-cotta tile summoned images of Italian hill towns. Florence's Villa
Palmieri yielded its wainscoting for the museum. "The Ringlings,"
wrote a biographer, "were helping to give Sarasota a new, Mediter-
ranean-inspired appearance." In 1925, Ringling dedicated one of his
hotels El Verona. Sadly, the Great Depression and Florida Land Bust
pricked Ringling's balloon.

Ringling's investments came crashing down in the late 1920s. He
died in bankruptcy in 1936, but he bequeathed to the State of Florida Ca'
d'Zan and the John and Mabel Ringling Museum of Art are considered
state treasures. Italian heirlooms continue to grace Sarasota. In 1950,
the Ringling estate purchased the Teatro di Asolo, an eighteenth-century Italian theatre where Eleanora Duse had once performed. The theatre was dismantled and reassembled in Florida.

The Ringling Art Museum in Sarasota, 1927.
Credit: Tampa/Hillsborough County Library.

Italian muralists and plasterers were not alone among the highly
skilled artists and artisans to bring their talents to Florida in the 1920s.
Florida's film industry, which was quite promising until the late 1920s,
attracted Italian musicians who played in the orchestra pits. Italian

musicians toured the state performing at forums such as the Italian Club theatre in Tampa, but also displaying their artistry at the finer auditoriums around the state. When the Saenger Theatre in Pensacola opened in 1935, the concert orchestra included several Italians: Frank Patalano, a cornetist, and Frank Marchese, a clarinetist. Prior to playing in the orchestra, he was the band master in Pensacola's 3rd Battalion Band. Marchese had been stationed with the 8th company band at Fort Barrancas.

If most Americans stigmatized Italian Americans as criminals, the story of Frank Angelo Croff is an instructive counter weight. Born in Italy in 1894, Croff (one suspects he changed his name) immigrated to America. A machinist and a baseball player, he joined the mass migration to South Florida where he became a motorcycle policeman. In May 1921, Croff was killed by a drunk driver while on duty.

The most prominent Italian-American politician in the 1920s and 1930s was Peter Tomasello Jr. The son of an immigrant who became a powerful lumber baron, Peter was born in West Florida at the turn of the twentieth century and moved to Okeechobee as a young man. A veteran of World War I, he achieved financial success by helping reorganize South Florida banks following the Florida land bust in 1926. Elected to the Florida House of Representatives in 1928, he served three consecutive terms and became speaker of the house during the 1933 legislative session. He was an unsuccessful candidate for governor in 1936. He died in 1961.

The luckiest Italians in 1920s Florida were Guido Rubiera, James Mirabella, Guy Rabedia, and a man identified only as Peppitona. They were sailors aboard the vessel *Hypnotist* that somehow had survived the worst hurricane to hit Tampa Bay in the twentieth century. In late October 1921, a category-3 storm (hurricanes were not given feminine names until 1953) roared upon the Gulf Coast, striking Anclote Key. The crew working for the Mirabella family clung to the rails of the foundering ship. The men had bonded and refused to put on life preservers when it was discovered that the crew was two preservers short. The *Hypnotist*, with its $7,000 haul, sank, but the men were somehow saved by a series of miracles and brave rescuers. Mirabella Seafood survived a century of hurricanes, mullet price wars, and pollution before it closed its doors in Tampa in 2003.

Sports

The 1920s also witnessed a feverish interest in sports in America and Florida. Young men found ample opportunities to play baseball, the most popular sport in the state. In Ybor City and West Tampa, cigarmakers and their sons played on factory teams, semi-pro leagues, and mutual and aid society clubs. Italian Club picnics featured long-distance races, boxing matches, and baseball games.

Each February and March, professional baseball teams came to Florida for extended spring training. Italian-American youth were bedazzled by the personal appearance of heroes they had only read about in the paper or heard about on the radio: Ernie Lombardi, Tony Lazzeri, Dolph Camilli, Sal Maglie, and Joltin' Joe DiMaggio. The son of Spanish emigrant parents, Tampa's Al Lopez made his major league in 1928 and became a role model for generations of Latins. Tony Cuccinello moved to Tampa as a young man and became a resident.

Boxing was also immensely popular in the 1930s, especially among Italian Americans. The boxing trainer and promoter Lou Viscusi spent many years in Tampa preparing athletes for the ring, while in Miami and Miami Beach's Fifth Street Gym, Angelo and Chris Dundee later worked as legendary trainers. Florida's Italian-American boxing fraternity includes "Kid" Bombero, Al DeRosa, Young Granado, Carl "Red" Guggino, Tony Leto, Jimmy Leto, Danny Nardico, Kid Pituso, and Johnny Minardi. Jake LaMotta, "the Raging Bull," opened a nightclub in Miami in the 1950s, a place depicted in the Martin Scorcese 1981 film.

Enterprise

Certain occupations became identifiable as Italian trades. Tailors, shoemakers, and fruit and vegetable vendors quickly became populated by Italians, partly because immigrants brought skills from the Old World, and partly because the public became convinced that Italians brought innate skills to these crafts.

One such skill was cutting hair. Barbering became a profession that Italian Americans populated. Setting up a barber shop was inexpensive, required relatively little schooling, and was easier work than swinging a pick. In a world and neighborhood where everyone got a hair cut every few weeks—and many a daily shave—barbering attracted lots of Italians who wanted security and place.

Barbers, too, joined their compatriots in the great exodus from Florida. By the 1960s, a favorite newspaper story featured Sal the barber, who was still cutting hair at age eighty and had not raised prices in decades. In 1980, the *St. Petersburg Times* highlighted 65-year-old Tony the barber, who for 26 years had cut hair along Central Avenue. Tony's father was an Italian immigrant who came to Brooklyn and learned to cut hair, a trade followed by his son. Tony Salmeri was old school: "no longhairs, no children, no women." He explained that wives had to wait outside. His take on hair salons: "Styling makes me laugh. It's the same thing as women of the night. Some charge $100 a night, and some charge $5. Hell, it's all the same." The price of a Tony Salmeri haircut in 1980: one dollar, less than he charged in New York City in the 1940s!

The 1920s and 1930s also produced some of Florida's most prominent Italian-American businessmen. Dominic (Pete) and Permetta Petrella migrated from Birmingham, Alabama, to Pensacola. Pete took a job with the Spearman Brewery. He later managed the Crystal Ice House, while his wife ran a fish market on T Street. Their grandson owns and operates Petrella's Italian Restaurant on 9 Mile Road.

1920's advertisement

Nicoló Geraci, a native of Contessa Entellina, Sicily, began his career peddling fruit and vegetables with a horse and cart in Tampa. He expanded his operations, building one of the state's first cold storage facilities. He incorporated his business as the American Fruit and Steamship Company.

Giuseppe Valenti landed in Tampa in 1894, a young man from Sicily. He, too, found work peddling fruits and vegetables. Upon his death, his son Joe "Blue Eyes" took over the modest business. He began purchasing vegetables from the rich hinterland. Eventually he helped organize the Tampa Wholesale Produce Market. By the 1940s Valenti was the largest wholesaler of tomatoes in the United States.

One of Florida's most successful corporations, Kash n' Karry boasts Italian roots. At the turn of the century, Salvatore Greco left Sicily for the cane fields of Louisiana. After a decade of toiling in Minnesota and Pittsburgh, he had saved a thousand dollars. Upon returning from Sicily with his new bride, he decided to invest his fortune in Tampa. In 1914, Salvatore Greco began peddling fruits and vegetables in Tampa. In 1922, he opened a small grocery store. By 1947, the enterprise was so successful that the Grecos opened their first supermarket, called the Big Barn Food Center. It eventually grew into today's Kash n' Karry, a major food chain in the South.

Son-in-law Frank Giunta helped expand the business from a single store to the third largest food retailer in Florida. Giunta's story is striking, as he explained in a 1980 interview. As a young child, he left the village of Santo Stefano in 1911 by mule cart to the port of Palermo. There a physician informed him that "sore eyes" prohibited his leaving. "Scared to death," he waved good-bye to his parents. On the road back to Santo Stefano, he encountered "*zingari*" [gypsies], who told him that Haley's Comet would bring doom. In Santo Stefano, enemies killed labor leaders and farmers. Fortunately, his vision improved and he joined his parents in Florida a year later.

The 1930s

The New Deal contributed to a cultural awakening in Florida. The federal government paid artists to paint murals and actors to stage theater. The only federal Spanish-language theatre in the United States occurred at Tampa's Centro Asturiano (an ornately decorated clubhouse that served Tampa's Spaniards from the province of Asturias). In Pensacola, the Federal Music Project sustained the local orchestra and other groups. In 1936, Pensacolans boldly produced the opera *Aida*. Elizabeth D. Vickers has written, "A most striking observation about the experience of the Great Depression in Pensacola is the depth of musical creativity that emerged despite the economic hardship. . . . Frank Marchese and his colleagues organized school bands under the umbrella of the WPA's federal Music Project." The Italian immigrant had studied music in Palermo and after serving in US military bands, was a familiar figure in Pensacola, working with student musicians. His son John also played with Pensacola's Philharmonic Orchestra. In the 1950s, Dr. John Venettozzi accepted the baton as conductor of the Pensacola Symphony.

Other Italian immigrants enriched Florida's music in the 1930s. Born in 1888, Ralph Sorrentino learned to play a variety of instruments in Catania, Sicily, his hometown. He obtained a job playing in an orchestra on an Italian cruise line. When the liner reached New York City, he auditioned for a position at a local theater, and was hired. He came to Florida while performing for the Ringling Brothers circus band. Sorrentino's sister resided in Apalachicola, Florida. While visiting the port city, he found out about an opportunity to play for the Chattahochee Mental Hospital band. He played there until the 1920s, when he moved to Panama City, where he settled down and performed.

When WPA writers compiled *Florida: A Guide to the Southernmost State* (1939), two events/individuals involving Italians made the 600-page book: Al Capone and Giuseppe Zangara.

In a state of dreams, easy money and fast tracks flourished. Almost from the beginning, Florida was a favorite place to export and incubate organized crime. In the 1948 film classic, *Key Largo*, Edward G. Robinson plays Johnny Rocco, an Italian gangster holed up in a Florida Keys' hotel during a hurricane. "After living in the US for more than 35 years they called me an undesirable alien," snorts Rocco. "Me! Like I was a dirty Red or something!"

Like George Washington's omnipresence at 250-year-old New England inns, Al Capone's presence pervades Florida. Sorting myth from reality has become a cottage industry in the search to validate Capone's presence in Florida. The Sunshine State has been especially attractive to mobsters and the underworld. Florida's tropical setting, lax regulations, and fluid mobility make it an ideal place to winter or invest.

Alfonso Capone first appeared at Miami Beach in the late 1920s. His reputation as *il capo di tutti capi* had been well established in Chicago. At the time, Miami Beach was recovering from a devastating hurricane two years earlier and a collapse in the real estate market, so the city had few scruples about allowing Jews in or keeping Italian gangsters out. Besides, illicit and legal gambling was already well established along the state's east coast. Released from prison in 1930, Capone chose to relocate to South Florida, purchasing a Palm Island mansion that had been originally built for St. Louis Brewers. He paid $40,000 for the Med Rev structure. If Capone expected to be ignored, he was wrong. The *Miami Daily News* campaigned to evict the intruder. Even the governor of Florida became agitated at his presence. Capone played the role of a prudish Midwesterner, simply glad to be resting his bones in the Florida sun. When asked his intentions, he claimed he hoped to join the local Rotary club. He listed his occupation as an "antique dealer." A neighbor testified that "every time a tire blew," she was certain that Chicago hit men were at work. In 1929, Capone went to prison, returning to the Magic City, only to be sentenced to jail once again in 1931. Miami couldn't live with him or without him. A 1940 *Miami Herald* headline announced, "Al Capone Comes Out of Retirement; Now Seen at Miami Beach Night Clubs." The 1941 WPA *Guide to Miami* recommended a visit to the Capone mansion to tourists. He died of syphilis in Miami in 1947.

Capone lives, and today is an even greater phenomenon than in the Roaring Twenties. His Spanish-style, two-story, un-air conditioned mansion at 93 Palm Avenue in Palm Island went on the market in 2006 for $6.9 million.

Other cities, towns, and resorts claim Capone pedigrees. In Whispering Hills, in Brevard County, locals are certain Capone murdered someone, or at least slept there. In 1930, Fort Lauderdale papers broke a story that Capone was planning to build a country manor and golf course at the confluence of the Hillsboro Canal and the Intra-coastal Waterway. The Hollywood Country Club was said to have been leased to the notorious mobster who operated it as a gambling casino. In remote Pasco County, long-time residents still believe that Capone was a frequent visitor to the Moon Lake Garden and Dude Ranch. The Jungle Country Club, a fashionable district hugging Boca Ciega Bay in Pinellas County, claims it served as a watering hole for Capone and friends.

In 1918, Capone and his soon-to-be bride had their first and only child: Albert Francis. The son resided in Miami, where he endured his surname and medical maladies. Ironically, Albert—called "Sonny"—befriended officers in the local police force and joined the department's pistol team. He and his mother ran a restaurant called The Grotto. In 1959 the Capones filed a one million dollar lawsuit against the producers of a TV show, *The Untouchables.* In another instance of art imitating life, the producer of the hit show was none other than Sonny's childhood friend, Desi Arnez. Albert Francis—he legally dropped the name Capone—died in 2004.

For all of the anxiety and fear, Al Capone's residency in Florida proved rather uneventful. Such was not the case of Giuseppe Zangara. In February 1933, Zangara, an unemployed bricklayer, attempted to assassinate President-elect Franklin D. Roosevelt at Miami's Bayfront Park. This sensational episode shocked an American public optimistic that FDR might offer some hope in a bleak world.

Zangara's rendezvous with destiny took many strange turns. Born in Ferruzzano, Calabria, Zangara immigrated to America in 1923. He worked as a mason in New Jersey. The Great Depression radicalized Zangara, who had nurtured a resentment against the rich and powerful since he was a boy. In 1900, the year of Zangara's birth, an Italian immigrant from Paterson, New Jersey, had shot and killed Italy's King Umberto. Zangara, too, tried to kill Victor Emmanuel III of Italy; in America he had contemplated killing Presidents Coolidge and Hoover. Suffering from terrible stomach pains, seeking sun and a fresh start, he migrated to Miami in early 1933, finding part-time work as a brick layer.

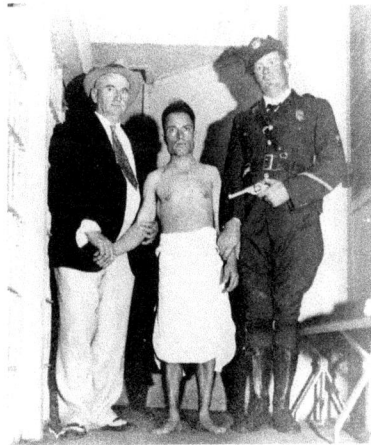

Italian immigrant Giuseppe Zangara in custody after attempted assassination of president-elect Franklin Roosevelt in Miami, 1933.

Credit: Florida State Archives.

The tortured immigrant read in the newspaper that

president-elect Roosevelt was scheduled to visit Miami on February 15, 1933. Convinced that he and he alone could make good this "propaganda by deed," Zangara went into a Miami Avenue shop to purchase a double-barreled, sawed-off shotgun. The proprietor, sensing the worst, refused to sell the weapon. Zangara walked across the street and bought a hammerless .32 caliber, five-shot revolver and ten bullets for $8. Bayfront Park was packed with 20,000 well-wishers as the five-foot, 100-pound assassin strained to see the patrician who had campaigned as a populist. The popular mayor of Chicago, Anton Cermak, had just made his way through the crowd to Roosevelt's convertible, when Zanzara, climbing atop a wooden chair, fired five shots. One bullet struck Cermak, who died of the abdominal wound three weeks later. Bullets also struck or grazed four persons, two seriously, but the president elect escaped unscathed. Some crime historians argue that Cermak, not Roosevelt, was the intended target.

A sensational trial followed. Sentenced to death, Zangara hectored the judge, "You give me electric chair. I no afraid of that chair. You're one of the capitalists. You is crook man, too." He was executed just thirty-three days after firing the fateful shot in Miami.

The war in Europe cast ominous shadows across the Sunshine State. By the late 1930s, journalists were duly noting the European connections in Florida: Greeks in Tarpon Springs, Bundles for Britain knitting parties in Winter Park, and Italian anti-fascists in Tampa. Pearl Harbor changed everything.

World War II and the 1950s

World War II served as a giant watershed for the sons and daughters of Italian immigrants. Cleaving ethnic America into distinct before and after eras, the war shattered the illusion of insularity, rallying all Americans to a common cause, and providing opportunities to millions of first- and second-generation Italians, Slavs, and Jews, allowing them entry into the middle classes, and provided possibilities of life outside the Northeast and the Midwest.

On the eve of Pearl Harbor, Italian Americans stood at a number of critical crossroads. They constituted America's largest white ethnic group, numbering 4.5 million first- and second-generation residents. Most lived in urban areas and industrial areas of the Northeast and Midwest. Italians had largely rejected the American South. To put demographics into perspective, Utica, New York, boasted more Italian residents in 1940 than the entire state of Florida. Tiny New Hampshire had about the same number of immigrants as Florida. Rhode Island, one-sixtieth the size of Florida, had twice as many foreign-born residents as Florida on the eve of war. The regions of the Old Confederacy lacked industry and conveyed a regressive, nativist attitude toward immigrants and Catholics. Ironically, the war would propel millions of Italian Americans to this once "benighted" South in the decades after WWII.

Pearl Harbor may have unified a divided America, but for many Italian families, the war posed many troubling questions. Patriotism and the draft suddenly meant that hundreds of thousands of young Italian Americans left Little Italies in Greenwich Village, Newark, and Chicago. Italian-American women took factory jobs, many of them moving to places offering lucrative jobs.

War dramatically altered the meaning of millions of immigrants residing in the United States. So-called "enemy aliens" from Germany, Japan, and Italy were required to register. The process had begun before Pearl Harbor. In 1940, authorities deported Alfio Scuderi, a fruit and vegatable grower residing in South Dade County. By April 1942, Italian "enemy aliens" were required to turn over items such as guns, cameras, and short-wave radios.

The South in general and Florida in particular welcomed millions of military recruits. Florida became an armed citadel during the 1940s, boasting almost two hundred military establishments. Camp Blanding, the Fort Lauderdale Naval Air Station, Eglin Air Field, the Avon Park Bombing Range, and others welcomed hundreds of thousands of young, impressionable recruits. More than a few were Italian Americans. Young Italian Americans were both fascinated and repelled by Florida's climate and mores. Some cursed the state's mosquitoes and insects; others were appalled at the region's treatment of Blacks. Many saw palm trees and tasted grits (*polenta senza sugo*) for the first time. Many also fell in love and married local girls. Overall, the military imposed a regimen upon young men accustomed to urban freedoms. Italian Americans ate the same food, prayed with the same chaplain, learned the same epithets, and wore the same uniform as Kansas farmboys, Montana cowboys, and Brooklyn rabbis.

War also allowed young Italian Americans to connect with *paesani* they had only heard about. The Allied invasion of Sicily brought young men to the villages of origin that parents and grandparents had left decades earlier. With a dateline, "Somewhere in Italy," *Tampa Tribune* reporter Gordon Grant accompanied several Italian Americans to their parents' villages. One, Gerald Randazzo, visited a country town near Naples to feast upon rabbit and straga wine. Captain Reinardo Pérez wrote his mother Catalina Reina in August 1943: "Yesterday, I took a 100 mile trip to the town where you were born. In a few minutes the place was full of relatives and everybody wanted to kiss me. I have never been kissed so many times in my life."

Tales abounded. Frank Adamo was a hero before he was a soldier. Born in Ybor City in 1893, Adamo grew up in Sicily when his father returned to the old country. Adamo immigrated to America where he worked as a cigarmaker in Tampa and Chicago. He learned English in Chicago and used his newfound passion for education to enroll in medical school. Dr. Adamo practiced medicine in Tampa in the 1920s and 1930s. Drafted into the army in 1941, he was stationed in the Philippines when Japan attacked the island fortress. He became one of America's first prisoners of war, surviving the Bataan death march and Japanese cruelty in Manila's Bilibid prison. He heroically performed surgeries at the prison hospital. Adamo met a friend from Tampa when he was liberated by American troops. When Adamo returned to Tampa, a grateful city named a street after the surgeon.

Lilian Toffaletti was born in 1916 in Port Tampa City. After attending Florida State College for Women, she and her sister Edith joined the WAACS. She accompanied General MacArthur when he liberated the Philippines.

To many veterans, the camaraderie and combat they experienced would be the most important events in their lives. Sixty-five years after the first draftees first encountered Florida, the veterans faithfully attend reunions in Jacksonville, St. Petersburg, or Orlando. A half-million Army Air Corps veterans trained in Miami Beach alone. Steve Acardi, who returned to visit old friends in 1999, was one such soldier. He was already in Miami Beach in 1941, working as a bus boy and waiter when, in 1942, he was drafted into the Army Air Corps (the predecessor of the Air Force). A physical fitness instructor, he remembered, "Being a good dancer, I had no problem getting dates."

John D'Albora of Cocoa, a veteran of World War I, also served as the first commander of the United States Coast Guard Auxiliary Flotilla Five. Comprised of Brevard County sailors and navigators, the unit patrolled the inland waterways around the Sebastian Inlet. Born in 1898 and a native of New York City, D'Albora was graduated from St. Johns College and migrated to Florida in 1924. He and his sons became leading grove owners, developers, and philanthropists.

Giuseppe Lupo occupies a special niche: the Sicilian-born resident of Coral Springs served in both World War I and World War II. Born in 1898, he joined the Italian army in 1916. In 1932, he came to New York City, working as a shoemaker. At age 44, he was drafted and sent to Fort Benning, Georgia. He and his wife, Ida, moved to Florida in 1977.

Many Italian Americans will rest in eternity in Florida military cemeteries. In 2007, the newest national cemetery opened in West Lake Worth in South Florida. One of the first to be laid to rest was Joseph Faggione, a World War II veteran who ran a Fort Lauderdale nightclub, Hotsy Totsy.

The war also brought home tragedy. Frank Campisi, a Panama City resident, learned that bombings had killed four members of his family in Avola, Sicily. In the Italian Club in Tampa, a war memorial lists the name of a dozen members who died for their country. A plaque in

Apalachicola honors the sacrifices made by locals, including the death of Christmas Castorino. Joe Caltagirone, a WWII veteran, recalls the war's grievous toll: "In my wife's neighborhood (Tampa), we lost three men. When the staff car would drive down the street, slowly looking for an address, the mothers or grandmothers on the porches would start screaming hysterically."

The home front also bristled with patriotism and volunteerism. The Italian Club in Tampa maintained a plaque of members serving in the military. Italian-American women rolled bandages for the Red Cross and volunteered for USO dances and scrap drives. Sisters Mary and Teresa Greco of Tampa worked at Drew and MacDill Fields during the war. They often bade goodbye to soldiers departing Union Station. Mary remembered, "When soldiers left on troop trains, I told them to sit on the left side, 'I'll leave the light on the porch.' Some of them never came back."

The greatest consequence of World War II occurred in the realm of greater social and economic expectations. Italian-American veterans took advantage of the G.I. Bill, allowing them to enroll in colleges or technical schools, purchase homes, and receive medical care. War had exposed to millions of impressionable youth the vision that life existed outside the old neighborhood. Many had been dazzled by the beaches and beauty of Florida. A good number of them would return, first as vacationers, and then later as residents and retirees.

Consider the case of Richard W. Fava. Born and raised in Roslindale, Massachusetts, he trained at the Fort Lauderdale Naval Air Station. His heroism on 24 July 1945 was awarded a Navy Cross. Bombs from his Grumman TBF-1 Avenger helped sink the Japanese battleship *Hyuga*. After military service in Korea and a successful business career, Fava and his wife Helen returned to Florida, retiring to DeLand in 1984. When Fava died in 2004, military aircraft flew over the museum in the "missing man" formation. In tribute, retired servicemen and town folk are restoring an Avenger aircraft at the DeLand Naval Air Station Museum.

Some GIs brought home more than memories from the war. Frank Fell brought a war bride from Italy. One of 11,000 such "war brides," Giuliana Baroni fell in love with an American GI who brought her to Perdido Beach (on the coastal border of Florida and Alabama). The

Florentine bride was horrified to discover how rural and hot and humid the Gulf Coast was. "I thought I had gone to hell," she recalled. Simply to shop, she had to travel twenty-five miles to Pensacola. She also learned a new cuisine. "Okra and corn were new to me," she confessed. She might have added new and terrifying creatures.

Some Italian Americans have left a legacy of their war memories in print. Patrick Caruso fought as a rifle officer with the marines on Iwo Jima. One-third of his company was wounded in the terrible campaign. Wounded, he returned to New Jersey to become an American history teacher. In 2001, he wrote *Nightmare on Iwo Jima* (Naval Institue Press). He spends several months a year in Bradenton, Florida.

J. S. Ripandelli typifies the migration to Florida of WWII veterans. A native of the Northeast, Ripandelli served in the 284th Engineering Combat Battalion during the war. He and his comrades fought their way from the Ardennes to the Battle of the Bulge to Nuremberg. On VE Day, First Lt. Ripandelli was in southern Bavaria in Himmler's hometown. After the war, he moved to Tallahassee, Florida, where he has been a stalwart supporter of Florida State University's acclaimed World War II Institute.

Frank J. Circelli was born in Cleveland and enlisted in the 82nd Airborne Division during World War II. At D-Day, he was in the thick of fighting and awarded the Purple Heart and Bronze Star for valor in action. Upon retiring as a painting contractor in 1959, he moved to Hollywood, Florida. He remained active in veterans' affairs until his death in 2007. He is buried in the Florida National Cemetery in Bushnell.

In the spring of 1946, Floridians read about an improbable rumor— that Italy's royal family was considering relocation to Tallahassee, Florida! Many years earlier, Lloyd C. Griscom, ambassador to Rome under President Theodore Roosevelt, had dined with the King and Queen of Italy. The patrician ambassador mentioned that he was considering retiring from the diplomatic service and getting into the newspaper business. King Victor Emmanuel III joked, "If I ever lose my job, will you give me one on your newspaper?" An exasperated Queen Elena asked, "What about me?" Griscom suggested that she could become the women's editor. Fate intervened. Griscom became the owner of the *Tallahassee Democrat*, the Italian royal family abdicated, and the Italian people renounced the monarchy.

The war and its aftermath connected Italians and Italian Americans once again. Italy's future was far from certain during and after the disastrous war. The Italian Left—socialists, communists, and syndo-anarchists—discredited and hounded in the 1930s, emerged as the heroic Popular Front in the 1940s. In the spring of 1948, Italians went to the polls to decide their political fate. Would the country be a monarchial republic, socialist state, or a democractic republic? The US State Department was deeply worried about the growing strength of the Left, so much so that officials orchestrated a campaign to urge Italian Americans to write *paesani* in the old country to vote for the Christian Democratic Party. The *Tampa Times* notes on April 1, 1948,

> Peter Maniscalco, former president and ex-secretary of the Italian Club . . . has given up all efforts to work during the approach of the important elections and is devoting all his time toward getting Tampa Italians to w r i t e their relatives and friends in Italy, urging them to stick by democracy.

Campaign by Mail

Tampa Italians Urge Friends to Oust Reds

By WILTON MARTIN
Times Staff Writer

The Italian people of Tampa want their mother country to vote Democratic in the April 18 elections, and they're doing something about it.

Already the Italian population here has mailed more than 2000 letters to relatives in Italy, particularly Sicily, urging them to spurn Communism, rally to the cause of Democracy and the free nations, and support the democratic candidates in this most crucial of all Italian elections.

It is estimated that Tampa's approximately 15,000 Italians are virtually without any trace of Communist sympathizers among them—not a single one is definitely known as such among the leaders of the local Italian colony. And they are proving it by their all-out efforts in behalf of democracy.

Peter Maniscalo, former president and ex-secretary of the Italian Club, who lives with his family at 1911 Carmen, and works as a bookkeeper and teacher, has given up all efforts to work during the approach of the important elections, and is devoting all his time toward getting Tampa Italians to write their relatives and friends in Italy, urging them to stick by democracy.

Publicity-shy because he says he is not seeking personal glory for his efforts, Maniscalo has, however, appeared before several large groups of Italians in public pleas for the letter writing campaign, and every day he visits scores of homes in the Italian section here personally explaining the importance of the letters. He has been leading the campaign in this manner for more than three months, and is working now even harder.

"Every effort has to be made," he said, "to get our relatives and friends over there to reject the Communists. Our colony is really going to bat for democracy's (See ITALIANS Page 6)

Tampa Times 1 Apr. 1948

Sunbelt Florida

Before 1940, Italian Americans in Florida were largely concentrated along seaport communities and in Tampa; after 1950, the pulse beat shifted to the East Coast. In the early 1950s, reporters began to notice perceptible changes in places like North Miami. Young GIs, attracted by cheap tract housing, began moving to the fast-growing city in Dade County. More than a few brought mothers and uncles and opened up Mom n' Pop Italian restaurants, bakeries, and motels. Many named their new stores after their old establishments in the Bronx or Chicago Heights.

From indentured servants working in semi-slave conditions to clear the wilderness to white-collar developers clearing orange groves to erect condominiums and malls, Italians have been involved in the construction of Florida. Interestingly, they are also intimately involved in the re-construction and re-design of Florida.

Social Networks

A plethora of housing projects and retirement complexes offered opportunities to Italian Americans eager to leave New York cold winters and take advantage of Florida's tax advantages and warm weather. Italian Americans began show up in Weston, Miramar, Century Village, Port Charlotte, Lehigh Acres, Spring Hill, Cape Coral, and Coral Ridge, places that did not even exist in 1940.

The greatest surge of Italian-American migration to Florida occurred in the decades after 1950. One manifestation of transplanted ethnicity is the rapid rise of Italian voluntary associations. As late as the 1940s, Florida had only one Sons of Italy Lodge (La Nuova Siclia Lodge

Display marking the OSIA Lodges at Port Everglades, Fort Lauderdale, Florida. At the Columbus Monument. 12 October 1992. Courtesy: Frank Cavaioli.

began in Tampa in 1924). By 2003, 37 such lodges existed in Florida; in 2007, 42 lodges had chapters in Florida. The places where Sons of Italy Lodges now thrive suggest volumes as to the nature of their beginnings and membership. Lodges exist in Cape Coral, Deltona, Spring Hill, and Port St. Lucie—communities that developed after 1950. The newest lodge is the Pembroke Pines order, chartered in 2007.

Retirement has brought a large number of Italian Americans to Florida. Sociologists might find research into this phenomenon worthwhile. Questions abound: What happens to ethnicity when one retires or moves to an area inhabited by large numbers of fellow ethnics from somewhere else? What is the relationship between class and ethnicity in Florida? Sons of Italy Lodges are found in some of the most modest places in Florida: West Tampa (Loggia Mona Lisa) and wealthiest communities (Jupiter's Cuore d'Italia Lodge and the Gulf Coast Italian Culture Society in Sarasota).

The Sons of Italy is merely one outlet for Florida's large Italian-American population. In 1976, so many Italians had moved to Florida that leaders organized the Florida Federation of Italian American Clubs at the Coffee Break Restaurant in Vero Beach. Clubs with names such as the Italian-American Women Today, the Italian Angels Motorcycle Brotherhood, the Gulf-Coast Italian Culture Society, and the Italian Cultural Society of Pensacola have taken root in Florida.

Just as immigration patterns were often the result of chain migrations, so, too, there seems to be patterns of migration from the North and Midwest to Florida. Large numbers of New Yorkers have settled along the state's southeastern Gold Coast. The Naples Italian-American Club reports that as many as 1,400 current and former Clevelanders attend ethnic festivals in Collier County.

Italian-American women have been especially active in their Florida networks. This may be a function of demography, since many such women are senior citizens, including many widows. In Clearwater, Le Itale-Americane di Oggi [Italian-American Women of Today] was organized in 1993. Every February 12, the group sponsors a popular festival in honor of San Gennaro.

Press

What Italian American exercised the greatest influence in late twentieth-century Florida? While Joe DiMaggio and Frank Sinatra frequently visited Florida (the former honeymooned with Marilyn Monroe in St. Petersburg while the latter crooned with the Rat Pack in Miami Beach), neither claimed residence in the Sunshine State. The distinction of cultural power broker must certainly go to an individual whose family's odyssey from Italy to New York City to Florida was part Horatio Alger, part Citizen Kane. In 1906, Fortunato Papa left Pasquarielli, Italy, for New York. He, like many of his countrymen, sought work in construction trades. He worked in Long Island sand pits and graduated to foreman, superintendent, and owner of the Colonial Sand and Stone Company. His marriage to Catherine Richichi bore three sons, including Generoso Jr. or Gene.

Generoso Papa anglicized the family name to Pope; however, the patriarch did not leave his Italian roots behind. He became one of the most powerful political figures in New York City ethnic politics, eventually becoming a member of Tammany's Democratic Committee. The New Deal and friendly mayors greatly enriched his construction business and influence. In 1928 he purchased the most important Italian-language newspaper in America, *Il Progresso Italo-Americano*. He was also expanding his power base outside Manhattan by becoming a champion of Italy's Duce, Benito Mussolini. Labeled an unrepentant Fascist by critics in the late 1930s, Pope pirouetted as an ardent patriot and anti-Communist after Pearl Harbor.

Generoso Pope Sr. died in 1950, leaving most of his fortune to charity. His namesake youngest son charted a very different journalistic career. A godson of mobster Frank Costello, a graduate of the Massachusetts Institute of Technology at age nineteen, Generoso Pope Jr. borrowed $75,000 to purchase the *New York Enquirer*, a failing newspaper with a circulation of 17,000. In the tradition of Charles Foster Kane, the young publisher converted the paper into a tabloid. Its focus upon the bizarre and titillating was so successful that Pope changed the name to the *National Enquirer* in order to reflect its appeal. In the 1960s, its lurid headlines leapt from supermarket check-out lines, and sales zoomed.

In 1971, Pope and the *National Enquirer* moved to Lantana, Florida, in Palm Beach County. The paper, with its five-million circulation, was fabulously successful, with Pope as its workaholic publisher-owner. The Pope of Palm Beach County was eccentric. He chain-smoked Kent cigarettes, drove an old Chevy, and did not have his first physical exam until age 45. When he died in 1988, his son Paul offered $1 million for information leading to his father's "suspicious" death. America Media Inc. purchased the *National Enquirer* for $413 million.

In the field of journalism, John Frasca won the Pulitzer Prize in 1966 in the category of local reporting. A New Englander and the son of Italian immigrant parents, Frasca was a marine lieutenant in World War II. Working for the *Tampa Tribune,* he investigated what appeared to be a routine story of a twenty-four-year-old who was arrested for robbing a Kwik Serve store in Mulberry, a depressed phosphate town in Polk County. Frasca's detective work exonerated the convicted man, earning the journalist kudos from his peers.

In 2008, Joseph Natoli was honored by the National Italian American Foundation with a special achievement award. A native of Brooklyn, Natoli followed the crowd to the Sunbelt, moving to Florida as a teenager. A graduate of the University of South Florida and an MBA from Nova Southeastern, he went to work for the *Miami Herald* (Knight Ritter) and rose through the ranks. By his fortieth birthday, Natoli became general manager and then president of the most important newspaper in Florida. Following assignments elsewhere, Natoli returned to Florida in 2006 to accept the position of chief financial officer at the University of Miami. The university's endowment recently topped the one billion dollar milestone. He has been an indispensable leader in South Florida's philanthropic circles, especially children's causes.

The *Orlando Sentinel*'s Mike Bianchi and *St. Petersburg Times'* John Romano have been highly touted for their sports writing. The *Times'* Paul Wilborn discovered his Sicilian roots when, in the 1990s, he returned to his grandparents' hometown in an award-winning column. Stephen Anthony Mondello began working on the *Pensacola News-Journal* in the 1960s as a trainee in the composing room. He represented a new generation of journalists who became more comfortable with the technological changes transforming the Fourth Estate. He spent four decades in his native Pensacola working at the *News-Journal.*

Politics

Historically, Italian immigrants shunned the political arena. More concerned with bread than ballots, many immigrants expected to return to the old country. In Italy, political participation was reserved for the privileged few. Filippo Licata served as a Tampa city councilman early in the twentieth century and Peter Tomasello Jr. was elected to the Florida legislature in the 1920s. The 1950s and postwar decades witnessed a dramatic rise in Italian-American political success.

Endowed with a famous name, Dante Bruno Fascell was witness to the century's great events: immigration and migration, boom and depression, hot wars and cold wars. Born in 1917 on his parents' Long Island dairy farm, his family moved to Coconut Grove, Florida, in 1925. His parents purchased the Miller dairy farm in south Dade County. A dairyman in New York, Fascell's father also delivered the milk. After graduation from Ponce de Leon High School, he received a law degree from the University of Miami, playing the clarinet in Depression-era dance bands to help with expenses. Commissioned a second lieutenant in May 1942, the five-feet, four-inch son of immigrants served under General Patton in Africa and Italy, where he earned three bronze stars. He often reminisced how as a lieutenant leading a truck convoy across the North African desert, he reflected, "If we ever get out of this thing, I'm going to find out a lot more about how the world works than I know now. . . . Wars are started by men, and I ought to be part of the process to help solve these things." He left the army as a captain.

Captain Fascell returned to Florida and began a remarkable political career. A legislative aide in Tallahassee in 1947, he was elected to the Florida Legislature in 1950. Four years later, his South Florida neighbors sent him to Washington. His congressional district ran from Coconut Grove to Key West. As a freshman congressman, he confronted a civil rights revolution. Pressured to sign the Southern Manifesto condemning the *Brown v. Topeka School Board* Supreme Court decision, Fascell demonstrated the moral courage to stand on principle. He served in the US House of Representatives from 1955 to 1993, chairing the powerful House Foreign Affairs Committee. He and fellow South Florida Congressman Claude Pepper formed a powerful alliance. President Clinton awarded him the Presidential Medal of Freedom in 1998. Dante Bruno Fascell died in November 1998. Bridges, beaches, and buildings bear his name, but it was his unblemished reputation for integrity that survives.

Nick Nuccio and Dick Greco, sons of Sicilian immigrants, each served two terms as mayor in Tampa in the decades of the 1950s, 1960s, and 1990s. Nuccio and Greco are regarded as two of the most beloved politicians the city of Tampa has produced. The popular Greco was succeeded in 2003 by Pam Iorio. The daughter of John Iorio, an Italian immigrant from Naples and an esteemed professor of English at the University of South Florida, Pam Iorio has enjoyed an extraordinary career in city/county politics. She was first elected county commissioner in her early twenties and then achieved a reform record as Hillsborough County Supervisor of Elections.

Nelson Italiano became an important power broker without ever having been elected. The son of Sicilian immigrants, Italiano was an outstanding athlete at Tampa's Hillsborough High in the late 1940s. His decision to attend Florida State University—the school was known as Florida State College for Women until 1947—was timely. He became one of that new coeducational school's first great football stars. But it was his friendship with fellow FSU student Reubin Askew—they dated and married sorority sisters—that changed his life. Upon graduation, Italiano launched a successful insurance company while Askew entered politics. When Askew was elected governor of Florida in 1976, he named Italiano his patronage chief.

While neither the most powerful nor the most famous Italian-American politician in Florida, "Captain" Tony Tarracino is certainly the most flamboyant office holder. A native of New Jersey, the son of a bootlegging father, the 32-year-old Tony moved to Key West in 1948, working as a shrimper and charter boat operator. In 1962 he purchased a Key West landmark, the "original" Sloppy Joe's, a watering-hole that Ernest Hemingway made famous decades earlier. Tarracino renamed the not-yet venerable establishment Captain Tony's Bar.

Frustrated by the changes sweeping Key West, Captain Tony ran unsuccessfully for mayor three times before being electing in 1989. He promised voters, "If I'm mayor, I'll tell you, we'll make the papers at least once a month. . . . That's what brings people here." He told one reporter, "All you need is a tremendous sex drive." Tony lost his bid for reelection, losing badly.

Broward County became the lodestar for countless Italian Americans who first voted for Fiorello LaGuardia and Frank Pastore in their youth. Alonso Gereffi migrated to Lauderdale Lakes in the 1960s and became city councilman until he was elected mayor, serving from 1973 to 1998. Anthony Scuotto was born in Brooklyn, a veteran who moved to Sunrise, Florida, in the 1980s. He joined the Sunrise Italian-American Civic association and participated in Broward County politics, serving on the Democratic party's executive committee. Scuotto died in 2007. Another New Yorker, Ed Puzzuoli, chaired Broward County's Republican Party. In 2007, Palm Beach county commissioner Tony Masilotti was sentenced to prison for embezzling public funds. Each spring, Florida legislators fear the name Dominic Calabro. He is closely associated with Florida TaxWatch, a non-partisan, non-profit government watchdog. "An almost native," Calabro moved to Broward County from New York at age eleven.

The most influential Italian-American politico in modern Florida may have been someone whose highest office was Deerfield city commissioner. Amadeo "Trinchi" Trinchitella earned a legendary reputation as a Broward County condominium power broker. From the moment he arrived in 1976, the Teamster-turned-condo commando advised Democratic candidates and rallied elderly Century Village voters to the polls. The transplanted New York retiree provided transportation and sample ballots to the 15,000 Century Village residents. Democrats frequently received 90 percent of that vote. When US Representative Robert Wexler met President Clinton, the chief executive quipped, "So you're Trinchi's congressman." When Wexler wondered how to defend President Clinton after the Monica Lewinsky affair, he asked Trinchi for advice. Former state attorney general Bob Butterworth eulogized at his 2005 funeral, "It's the end of an era."

Amadeo Trinchitella was a witness to a political revolution. When he arrived in Florida in 1976, the Sunshine State was solidly Democratic. The only Republican-elected governor in a century was promptly replaced by a progressive Democrat, and Florida helped elect the Georgia Democrat Jimmy Carter to the White House. Dramatically and triumphantly, the Republican Party mounted a steady assault upon a state once part of the Solid Democratic South. Thirty years after Trinchi's arrival, both the Florida House and Senate, the governor, every cabinet position, and one US senator were Republicans. When Dante Fascell ran for Congress in 1954, no Republicans sat in the Florida delegation. By 1998, Florida became the first southern state in the twentieth century with a Republican governor and legislature.

The latest Italian-American congressman to achieve power in Florida is John Mica. The Republican represents Florida's Seventh Congressional district, a belt ranging from Orlando to Jacksonville. He is finishing his seventh term as congressman.

Historically, Italian-American politicians in Florida had been Democrats: witness Fascell, Nuccio, and Tomasello. Beginning in the 1980s, a new wave of Italian-American politicians ran successfully for office. The 2000 Florida Legislature included six Italian Americans: Nancy Argenziano, Dunnellon; Mike Fasano, New Port Richey; Heather Fiorentino, New Port Richey; Jack Latvala, Palm Harbor; Jim Sebesta, St. Petersburg; and John Morroni, Clearwater. All represent Gulf Coast districts; all are Republicans. Italian Americans serving in the 2008 legislature included Senator Gwen Margolis and Representatives Carl Domino, Richard Glorioso, and Maria Sachs.

Education

Italian immigrants brought a historic distrust of formal education. Struggles with educators, truant officers, and the urban bureaucracy characterized the early decades of the twentieth century. To most Americans, college was a privilege before the 1950s; to Italians who associated blue-collar jobs with success, higher education was even more improbable.

In Florida, the story is complicated. In Tampa, immigrant parents recognized that by the 1930s, the cigar industry offered few opportunities for their children. When I interviewed elderly Italians, many spoke of their parents' wonderment at the "freeschoola." I could not find such a word in the dictionary, but quickly realized they meant the free school, the public schools were open to all. When Tony Pizzo entered the University of Florida in the early 1930s, he joined Sigma Iota fraternity, composed of fifty Latins, mostly Italian from Tampa. But Florida's poorly funded educational system, unlike New York, Pennsylvania, or Illinois, offered limited opportunities for its students. Until 1947, Florida's white male students had only one option to attend a four-year public college, the University of Florida in Gainesville.

Enrico Tamburini was one of the first Italian-born professors to teach in Florida. Born in Pesaro, Italy, in 1894, he arrived at Winter Park, Florida, in 1936 to teach cello at Rollins Conservatory of Music. He taught from 1936 to 1938 and then took a leave of absence to return to Italy. One curiously wonders what happened to the cellist.

Higher education in Florida exploded in the 1960s and in the decades following. Lawmakers established new public universities in Tampa, Orlando, Miami, Jacksonville, Pensacola, and Boca Raton. Attracted by year-round sunshine and the informality of dress and admissions, many New Jersey and New York Italian-American students enrolled at Florida State University and the University of Florida.

If Italian students were relatively rare before the GI Bill and post-war decades, Italian professors were even more precious. Beginning in the 1960s, as higher education became a growth industry and a ticket to the middle class, significant numbers of Italian Americans entered the professorial ranks. Young PhDs flocked to Florida to teach in the fastest growing state in America.

John Iorio participated in this vanguard. Born in 1925 outside Naples, Italy, he immigrated with his parents to New Jersey. When he entered public schools, John did not know any English. He quit high school to become a paratrooper at age seventeen. Because of his birthplace in Italy, authorities investigated the young volunteer, wishing to know about his loyalty and leanings. In a tableside ceremony, an FBI agent peered into Iorio's eyes and asked, "Young man, would you be willing to bomb your home town?" Unruffled, Iorio responded, "What, are you crazy? Why would I want to bomb Trenton, New Jersey?" He joined the 7th Airborne and fought at the Battle of the Bulge.

The GI Bill opened doors for Iorio he could not have imagined. A working-class ethnic, he first finished high school and then enrolled at Columbia University. After teaching at Colby College in Maine, he heard about a new university that had just opened in Tampa: the University of South Florida. He recalled the excitement of the period: "The 1960s after all loosened up an awful lot of things. It created fears, but it also created new parameters of behavior, of dress, of thinking, of attitudes." Arriving in 1963, he spent more than thirty years as a much beloved and accomplished professor of English. His daughter, Pam Iorio, serves as mayor of Tampa. John Iorio passed away in February 2007.

John Lombardi came from a distinguished family of educators. His mother worked as a college librarian while his father was a pioneer in the California community college system. John earned a PhD at Columbia University and became a leading authority and the author of seven books in Latin American history. In 1990, he assumed the presidency of the University of Florida, where he served as a forceful and energetic leader until 1999.

Anthony Catanese served as president of Florida Atlantic University through the 1990s, transforming it into a major research university that was on the cusp of attaining research-one status before leaving to head up the Florida Institute of Technology in Melbourne.

In 1998, Ray Ferrero Jr. was named Nova Southeastern University's fifth president. The son of Italian immigrants had achieved success as a trial attorney—having served as president of the Florida Bar—and had just turned age 64. In June 2008, Ferrero celebrated his tenth anniversary at the private institution, whose Broward County enrollment has reached 27,000 students. In ten years, Nova Southeastern University has increased its enrollment by 62 percent and added 24 degree programs. A St. Johns University graduate and a former Marine Corps captain, Ferrero received his law degree from the University of Florida and moved to Fort Lauderdale in the early 1960s.

In 1966, Florida State University established a study center in Florence, Italy. For four decades, the center has allowed thousands of Floridians to appreciate the benefits of study abroad. The Palazzo Alessandrini, a fifteenth-century villa, provides an elegant setting for the Florentine campus. For over two decades, Victor Carrabino served as the center's indefatigable director. Mark Pietralunga, once assistant director of the FSU study center and the Victor Oelschlager Professor of Modern Languages at Florida State University, has also established an impressive reputation for the study of modern Italian literature.

A New Yorker, John Vennettozzi earned his doctorate in music at Florida State University. Affectionately called "Dr. John," he originally came to teach at Pensacola Junior College. In addition to teaching, he also played and later conducted the Pensacola Symphony. His energy was boundless, as he also directed the choir and played the organ at the local Presbyterian Church. One of the early choir members was future Florida governor Reubin Askew. In the 1970s, he became the director in charge of the new West Campus of Pensacola Community College.

John Paul Russo is Professor of English and Director of Graduate Studies at the University of Miami. A Fulbright scholar and a specialist in modern British and American cultural studies, Russo edits the journal *Italian Americana* and is the award-winning author of *I.A. Richards: His Life and Work* and *The Future Without a Past: The Humanities in a Technological Society*. A colleague of Russo, Robert Casillo has dedicated much of his intellectual activities to Italian-American cinema. Most recently, he published *Gangster Priest: The Italian American Cinema of Martin Scorsese*.

Phil Cannistraro was one of the towering figures in Italian history. He arrived at Florida State University in the 1970s and taught there until he accepted a position at Drexel University and, then later, as chair in Italian-American studies at the City University of New York. He was one of the leading scholars of Fascist Italy. His death in 2005 was a terrible loss to the profession and his many friends.

Robert Cassanello represents the future of Florida history in a state where it seems almost everyone is from somewhere else. An assistant professor of history at the University of Central Florida, his Italian roots go back to Genoa, Tuscany, and Sicily. The family settled in the Northeast before moving to Dania, Florida, in the 1970s. Cassanello received his doctorate at Florida State University.

In 2004, Paolo Giordano became Chair of the Department of Modern Languages at the University of Central Florida. He is a prolific author, a co-founder and editor of *Voices in Italian Americana*, and the author and editor of many books, most notably a study of Joseph Tusiani and the critically acclaimed *From the Margin: Writings in Italian Americana,* which he co-edited with Fred L. Gardaphé and Anthony Julian Tamburri.

A prominent scholar of Italian and Italian-American studies, Anthony Julian Tamburri left Purdue University in 2000 to chair the Department of Languages and Linguistics at Florida Atlantic University in Boca Raton. The Connecticut native also served as Associate Dean for Graduate Studies in Arts and Letters. Tamburri's efforts to establish a relationship with Florida's Italian-American communities proved especially successful. A co-founder of Bordighera Press, Tamburri made Florida Atlantic University and Boca Raton an Italian literary and publishing center. In 2006, he left to become the dean of the John D. Calandra Institute at Queens College of the City University of New York.

Emanuel L. Paparella was Professor of Italian at the University of Central Florida and Florida Atlantic University. A PhD from Yale University, Paparella has written about the philosopher Giambattista Vico. He also served as the director of the University of Central Florida's Urbino summer program.

George Pozzetta taught at the University of Florida for a quarter century, 1970–1994. He was a brilliant historian, a prolific author, and a beloved colleague. He co-authored *The Immigrant World of Ybor City* and edited the *Florida Historical Quarterly.* Pozzetta, along with Tamburri, LaGumina, Cavaioli, and Femminella, were presidents of the American Italian Historical Association (AIHA).

Christopher D'Elia, a native of Connecticut, received his PhD in Zoology from the University of Georgia. Following post-doctorate posts at UCLA and the Woods Hole Oceanographic Institute and teaching positions at SUNY Albany, he became a professor of environmental science and policy and associate vice chancellor for research and graduate studies at the University of South Florida, St. Petersburg.

Frank Biafora represents a young generation of Italian-American educators. His grandfather emigrated from San Giovanni di Fiore, Campania, to New York. A tailor, he realized New York City already was bursting with Italian tailors, so he migrated to Morgantown, West Virginia, where he found a calling and a bride. Born in 1965 in West

Virginia, Frank Biafora moved with his family to Daytona Beach in 1976. A graduate of the University of Florida, he received his doctorate in sociology from the University of Miami. After serving as dean at St. John's University in New York, he became dean of Arts and Sciences at University of South Florida, St. Petersburg in 2007. A specialist in juvenile delinquency and a Fulbright scholar in Vietnam, he is married to LeaAnn Bustamante. Ms. Bustamante is a registered nurse and health-care administrator.

Dick Puglisi holds the Stavros Chair in Free Enterprise and Economic Development at USF Tampa, where he directs the Gus A. Stavros Center. The son of American-born Mary Christina Nuccio and Joseph Salvatore Puglisi, a Sicilian immigrant who settled in Tampa, Puglisi, born in Tampa in 1942, credits much of his success to the work ethic imbued by his family and the opportunities afforded by public education. After his undergraduate degree from newly opened University of South Florida, Puglisi received his PhD from the Georgia State University. He returned to Tampa and began his college teaching career at USF in 1969 in the College of Education. His many honors include the Freedoms Foundation Award of Excellence in Private Enterprise Education.

Rev. Monsignor F. M. Casale has served as president of Miami's St. Thomas University since his appointment in 1994. He received his Masters of Divinity from the Immaculate Concepcion Seminary in Darlington, New Jersey.

After completing his medical degree at the University of Milan, Camillo Ricordi immigrated to America for several prestigious research positions. In 1993, he moved to Miami where he has held the Stacy Joy Goodman Chair of Medicine at the University of Miami. An international authority in cell transplantation, Dr. Ricordi is founder and president of the Cell Transplant Society and co-founder of the National Diabetes Research Coalition.

In 2008, officials in Indian River County tapped Harry La Cava as superintendent of education. La Cava, a graduate of the University of Florida, holds a doctorate from Nova Southeastern University and has spent thirty years in the Broward County school system. A fellow Broward County educator, David M. Piccolo, was a finalist for the Indian River County position.

Few Florida Italian Americans exercised the clout of Pat Tornillo. The son of Italian immigrants who settled in New Jersey, Pat was born in 1921. A veteran of WWII and a graduate of Seton Hall University, Tornillo moved to Miami in 1956. He began teaching at Biscayne Gardens Elementary School. Upon joining the Dade Classroom Teachers' Association, Tornillo rose through the ranks, becoming president of the powerful union in 1962. He gained fame—and notoriety—after leading teachers in a heated 1968 strike. By the mid-1980s, he led the Florida Teachers' Union, a position he held for two decades. He later admitted to looting the union of millions of dollars. He went to prison and died in 2007.

Understandably, Florida has become a popular place for retired academics. A remarkable constellation of retired New York Italian-American professors reside in Broward and Palm Beach counties. In 1966, many of these individuals were present at the creation of the American Italian Historical Association at Staten Island. Today, they call Florida home. Frank Femminella, a sociologist at SUNY Albany, resides in Royal Palm Beach. Sal LaGumina, a pioneering historian of the Italian-American experience and a professor at Nassau Community College, winters at Pompano Beach. Frank Cavaioli, also a gifted chronicler of Italian Americans and former professor at Farmingdale State, SUNY, resides at Pompano Beach. Cavaioli, a former president of AIHA, has delved into the history of Florida, writing a number of books about Broward County communities and places. Frank Samponaro retired to Sarasota after teaching history many years at the University of Texas of the Permian Basin. A scholar of the Mexican Revolution, he is now involved with the Yale Club of the Suncoast. Peter Sammartino, founder of Fairleigh Dickinson University in New Jersey, owned a condo in Palm Beach and was actively involved with local cultural studies until his death in 1992.

Neil Euliano, a professor of anesthesiology in the School of Medicine at the University of Florida, and the president of Convergent Engineering in Gainesville, has received acclaim for his invention of a medical ventilator and a fetal heart monitor. In 2005, he endowed a million-dollar chair at the University of Central Florida. The Neil Euliano Distinguished Chair in Italian Studies represents a seminal achievement in the state of Florida.

Florida was once considered beyond the pale for historians study-ing Americans and Italian Americans. Today, Florida is an irresistible subject for popular sociologists and serious academics. For example, the American Italian Historical Association held its annual meeting in Florida in 2003 at Boca Raton, returning just three years later, to Orlando in 2006.

Encouraging signs indicate that the teaching of Italian language and traditions to the young will endure. *Il Circolo,* the Italian Cultural Society of the Palm Beaches, annually recognizes local students who have excelled in the study of Italian. In 2005, the Sarasota Order of Sons of Italy donated $1,600 to a talented Riverview High school teacher, Bridget Coughlin, who used the scholarship to spend a month studying in Italy. The National Italian American Foundation has also touched teachers and students in Florida with scholarships and awards.

Law

John Gale compiled a distinguished judicial career in South Flor-ida. The administrative judge of the 11th Judicial Circuit Court in Miami, he was highly decorated for his activities in the community. Born in Malden, Massachusetts, in 1927, Gale served with Army Intelligence during World War II. Following law school at the University of Miami, he began a legal career that spanned three decades. In 2005, he was awarded the Ellis Island Medal of Honor by the board of directors of the National Ethnic Coalition of organizations. He was a founding father of the National Italian American Foundation and was knighted by the Republic of Italy as Cavaliere Commandante for his contribu-tions to the law and society. He was also once considered for the posi-tion of commissioner of baseball. Retired, Gale now heads Private Judges Inc., an arbitration and mediation service.

Judge Peter R. Palermo's story is a compelling tale of heroism and persistence. Born in Pittsburgh, the son of Italian immigrants from Portanapoli, Palermo attended local schools and graduated from Penn State. One of the first draftees, he entered the US Army but served in the Army Air Corps. Providentially, he was sent to Miami Beach for basic training. "All of Miami Beach was taken over by the Army Air Corps," he explained. His barracks was the romantic-sounding Art

Deco hotel, Fadigo Court. After serving in some of the toughest fighting in Italy, he did manage to secure an Italian driver and translator to
take him and see his relatives near Naples. "They treated me like a
hero coming home." For his actions, Captain Palermo was awarded the
Bronze Star and six battle stars. In 1947, he enrolled at the University
of Miami Law School. While a law student, he was elected mayor of
West Miami, a position he held for three consecutive terms. President
Richard Nixon appointed him a federal judge in 1971. Today, he continues to serve as Senior Magistrate Judge of the US District Court in
Miami. When asked if he was the oldest active judge in Miami, he
replied, "I am the oldest judge in the whole damned country!" As
judge, the son of immigrants presided over the two largest groups of
citizens sworn in at any one time in the history of the country, part of
a half-million new citizens he has welcomed.

William J. Castagna and Richard A. Lazzara also serve as judges for
the US District Court in the Middle District of Florida. Castagna was
born in Philadelphia in 1924. A veteran of World War II, he practiced
law in Clearwater, Florida, from 1950 to 1979, when President Jimmy
Carter appointed him a federal judge. Richard Lazzara was born in
Tampa in 1945 and attended Loyola University and then law school at
the University of Florida. Following private practice, he served on the
13th Judicial Circuit of Florida, 1988–1993, and then Appellate Judge
from 1993–1997. In 1997, President William Clinton appointed him US
District Judge.

The title of his autobiography, *Mob Lawyer* (1994), tells much about
the life and career of Frank Ragano. Born in 1923, the son of a Sicilian
emigrant who ran a small store in Tampa, Ragano fought in the US Army
during World War II, earning a Bronze Star for his valor in Germany. After
his education, he clerked for the Florida Supreme Court. In 1948, he represented his most important client, alleged Tampa mafia boss, Santo
Trafficante. He later defended Jimmy Hoffa. He and Trafficante visited
Cuba frequently. He became friends with US Senator John Kennedy,
purportedly the fictional womanizing US senator depicted in *Godfather
II*. Convicted of income tax evasion on two occasions, he lost his legal
license in the 1970s. By 1984 he was defending Trafficante in a racket-
eering case. His sensational autobiography insisted that American mob

bosses had assassinated President Kennedy.

A list of the sheer number of Italian judges, lawyers, and physicians in Florida would resemble a phone directory. One family deserves mention. Spoto was a prominent name among the Sicilians who left Santo Stefano for America. Many settled in Tampa. Literally, so many Spotos came to Tampa that the name is now rare in southern Sicily. Spotos have also been exceptionally successful, especially in the legal and medical professions. I.C. Spoto was one of the first Italian judges in America. He was followed by Nick Falsone, Rene Zacchini, Dick Greco Jr, Sam Pendino, and Denise Pomponio.

Enterprise

In the 1980s, the Washington-based National Italian American Foundation (NIAF) began organizing chapters in Florida. The individual behind the organizing impetus of NIAF was the irrepressible Jeno Paulucci. Born in Minnesota's Iron Range country in 1918, Paulucci, the son of Italian immigrants, made his first fortune in his 20s with his risky investment in Chinese food. Early in his career, he encountered Central Florida's celery fields. The flamboyant founder of Jeno's Pizza Rolls, Chun King, Luigino's, and scores of other brands purchased thousands of acres of real estate in Central Florida and moved his corporate headquarters from Duluth, Minnesota, to Sanford. Paulucci, a moving force in NIAF, also developed the up-scale Heathrow community in Seminole County.

Italian-American success stories appear regularly in modern Florida. Antonio Rossi was born in Sicily and immigrated to America at age twenty-one. He began as a green grocer in Miami who discovered that customers enjoyed having their oranges and grapefruit cut into sections. He was soon packing gift fruit boxes for Macy's of New York. In 1947, he founded Tropicana, a Florida fruit-packaging firm that also delivered fresh juice to homes. In 1954, Tropicana scientists pioneered a pasteurization process that allowed pure chilled juice to be shipped in glass bottles. In 1978, Rossi sold the firm to Beatrice Foods for $425 million. He resided in Bradenton until his death in 1993.

Lou Perini was a larger-than-life figure. Born in Massachusetts in 1904, he took over his father's construction business at age twenty-one. His firm flourished during the New Deal and WWII. In 1941 Perini and Guido Rugo, two of the "Three Steam Shovels," purchased the Boston Braves of baseball's National League. In 1953, he moved the struggling franchise to Milwaukee, where it became the toast of baseball. Perini's greatest coup, however, was not signing Henry Aaron, but purchasing 5,500 acres of Palm Beach County real estate for $4.35 million. He became one of southeast Florida's great developers, the founder of the villages of Palm Beach Lakes. Perini died in West Palm Beach in 1972.

Few developers have made more dramatic entrances and exits than the Berlanti brothers. The family originally settled in rural Connecticut where the sons milked cows and weeded orchards. Louis Berlanti, the oldest son, first achieved success in the construction business. The New Deal and World War II enriched the family/company coffers. By the 1950s, the Berlanti Overseas Corporation was one of the largest construction firms in the Northeast, overseeing hundreds of millions of dollars in projects. Even though the company lost $5 million when Castro took control of Cuba, the brothers were attracted to the Florida Gulf Coast.

In 1959, the Berlanti brothers purchased 2,000 acres of land, much of it submerged, in lower Boca Ciega Bay in Pinellas County. The battle to win legal approval to dredge and fill on a colossal scale was almost as challenging as the engineering demands. The family persevered, eventually investing $50 million into what became known as Tierra Verde. Planners envisioned a grand city on the gulf that would be home to 50,000 residents seeking the good life. On 16 August 1963, about the time the first lots were being sold, Fred Berlanti's twin-engine Beechcraft crashed, killing all aboard. Thirty years later, hints of foul play still circulate. The dream of Tierra Verde endures as one of the great development successes.

Another prominent developer was Pasquale J. Sergi. The son of Italian immigrants who resided in New York's Lower East Side, Sergi was a neighbor to Al Smith. His boyhood friends included Irving Berlin, George Jessel, Al Jolson, Eddie Cantor, and Jimmy Durante. His mother fully expected young Pasquale to become a priest, but he instead became a construction boss. He helped build the Chrysler building. In

1924, Pasquale came to St. Petersburg. He directed his energies into purchasing beachfront property from Sarasota to Pass-a-Grille, at a time when the beach was largely undeveloped and isolated. He acquired the land that later became the fashionable Lido Beach. He was instrumental in getting telephone service for the beaches. There, he welcomed Joe DiMaggio and "Two Ton" Tony Galento. He died in 1954.

In the 1992 film *Glengarry Glen Ross*, Al Pacino plays the fast-talking Ricky Roma, who sells swampland in Florida. In real life, Italian Americans poured into Florida to sell homes in places like Deltona and Spring Hill. One of the earliest and most successful real estate developments was Cape Coral, a 1950s city built upon the banks of the Caloosahatchee River in Southwest Florida. Pioneer salesmen included Edward Pacelli and Joseph Maddlone. One of the major contractors for the massive project was Clarence Duffala of the Duffala Construction Company.

Broward County was an inviting target for developers in the years after World War II. Boasting a landmass of 1,320 square miles, Broward's 1950 population of 83,933 was underwhelming. Developers with grand ambitions rushed to the Sunshine State. In 1946, a team of developers formed Coral Ridge Properties. Joseph Taravella helped change the face of Broward County from Fort Lauderdale to Pompano Beach. In 1953, Taravella's Coral Ridge Properties purchased the Galt Mile, almost 2,500 acres of unoccupied waterfront property.

Charles Joseph Chiapetta, the only son of seven children born to Italian immigrants, was born in 1914 in Greenwich, Connecticut. He and his wife moved to South Florida in 1948, where he became involved in the postwar boom. Charles developed and built Hollywood Pines. In 1958, he moved to Pompano Beach, where he developed Pompano Estates, as well as other commerical projects. He also owned Love Realty for fifty years. Chiappetta passed away in March 2007. One of Chiapetta's associates and rivals was Joseph Balistreri. A native of Milwaukee, Wisconsin, Balistreri moved to Pompano Beach and became a prominent realtor. He passed away in June 2006.

To Art Furia, Italian-American relationships are both personal and business. A Miami attorney, Furia was the son of Italian immigrants who settled in Philadelphia. In 1980, he joined Miami's law firm of Gunster Yoakley. He became president of Miami's Italian Chamber of

Commerce and in 1995 was appointed Italy's *ufficiale legale* [official legal representative] for the Southeast. It was his responsibility to assist the Versace family after the murder of Gianni Versace in South Beach. He has also led Florida Governors Martínez and Bush to trade missions to Milan and Rome. Today, Italy is the third most important European trade partner after the United Kingdom and Germany and the fourth biggest client at the Port of Miami. Italian marble and tile, apparel and wine have become trendy features at upscale South Florida homes and cafes.

In 2008, the National Italian American Foundation honored Franco Nero for his many accomplishments. He serves as president and CEO of the Beacon Council, an organization devoted to international economic development. A native of New Jersey, he became the youngest mayor in North Plainfield, New Jersey's history. Nero moved to Jacksonville in 1991 where he served as deputy mayor for economic development. Since moving to Miami, he has served on almost every committee dedicated to international trade and development. He has been especially active in encouraging trade and alliances between Italy and Miami/Dade County.

Like most of the successful Italian entrepreneurs in Florida, paths to success were often convoluted. Carlo Toppino left Italy for New York City. He and his wife Orsalina raised five sons. A World War I veteran, Toppino moved his family from New York to a place that was about as far removed from metropolitan life as possible: Marathon, Florida, on one of the islands in the archipelago of islands between the mainland and Key West. In 1940, the Toppinos moved to Key West, where Toppino & Sons became one of the areas largest construction firms. Massive federal investments in Monroe County and Key West during the 1930s and 1940s helped make the Toppino family very wealthy.

The Sacino family, the first name in formal wear, also established businesses and residence in Florida. A native of Potenza, Italy, Giovanni Sacino immigrated to Fitchburg, Massachusetts. In 1916, he opened a tailor's shop, an occupation of so many Italians. Like many residents of the Northeast, he grew tired of the winters and moved to St. Petersburg in 1949. Nicknamed the Sunshine City, St. Petersburg was arguably the most popular retirement destination in America in the 1940s, '50s, and '60s. Sacino was not ready to retire, so he opened a men's clothing store at the Derby Hotel in St. Petersburg. In 1952, he decided to branch into the formal wear rental business. In the "I-Like-Ike" decade, his business thrived. Today, Sacino Formalwear boasts scores of stores in Florida and the Southeast.

When Margaret Ghiotto died in 2006, generations of customers grieved. The Florida native founded and owned Rogers' Christmas House in Brooksville. She had recently sold the establishment for $1.5 million.

Edward Netto, born in Santa Clara, California, in 1919, came to Vero Beach as a serviceman in World War II. An aviation metal-smith, he served at the Vero Beach Naval Air Station. He met and married a local girl, and chose to remain in Indian River County after the war. Indian River County's pristine beaches had barely been touched; the entire county's population was less than 12,000 in 1950. The Netto Construction Company became a leading builder on the East Coast of Florida in the boom decades to follow.

M.C. Minella also left his imprint upon Florida's East Coast. An emigrant from Naples, Minella spent his youth in Kentucky, coming to Cocoa Beach in 1927. He was involved in construction and real estate, and in 1959 relocated to Vero Beach. He was instrumental in constructing the Heather Apartments and Lounella Apartments.

Andy Cagnetta is president of Transworld Business Brokers in Fort Lauderdale. He purchased the firm in 1997 and today it employs 32 brokers who consult well more than 100 businesses annually.

Anthony Pugliese III and Fred DeLuca have planned one of Florida's most ambitious developments. These fabulously successful business-men seek to transform one of Florida's most obscure places, Yeehaw Junction, into the state's "first eco-sustainable city . . . a bio-technolog-ical hub, with 40 miles of navigable lakes, a sustainable energy source, and 150,000 people." Pugliese, a real estate tycoon, and DeLuca, founder of Subway restaurants, face formidable opposition and opti-mistic support for their grandiose proposal to transform what has been land for cattle and Florida Turnpike commuters into a community they call Destiny.

"Buster" Agliano was neither the wealthiest nor most powerful Italian American in modern Florida, but he can lay claim to one distinction: he was Ybor City's last fishmonger. He came from a distinguished line of fishermen and fishmongers. His grandfather, Sebastiano Agliano, left Sicily for Tampa, selling fish by push cart to make a living. By the time he died in 1938, Agliano owned a fleet of ships and stores.

Photo credit: Gary Mormino, 2000.

"Buster" was born in 1935 and, upon graduation from his beloved University of Florida, expected to take over Agliano & Sons Fish Company from his father Joseph. He did, but the business had shrunk. Foreign competition hit old businesses hard. He explained that Americans no longer care where their fish comes from; they don't even know the name of the kid at Publix who sells them grouper. Buster maintained the store on Seventh Avenue in Ybor City because it allowed him to gossip with old friends. Buster Agliano, Ybor City's last fishmonger, died in 2003.

Louis Buccino left Philadelphia in 1993, moving to Orlando where he worked for Lockheed Martin Information Systems. In 1998, he accepted a position as director for community relations and public affairs at Citicorp/Citigroup. His grandfather, Vincenzo Buccino, emigrated from Campania, Italy, in 1891, settling in New Haven, Connecticut.

The DeBartolo family is an American success story with roots in the hardscrabble town of Youngstown, Ohio. Antonio Paonessa left Italy for the Ohio steel mills, but died a few months before his son Edward John was born in 1919. His stepfather Michael DeBartolo, a mason, adopted him. As a young man, Edward worked at his father's construction business. He graduated from University of Notre Dame and returned to Youngstown where he became president of the construction firm. Youngstown boomed during and after the war, and the DeBartolo Corporation prospered.

Edward DeBartolo keenly observed the changing demographics and residential/shopping patterns of post-war America. He witnessed a decline of Rustbelt downtowns and the ascent of suburbia, building strip malls, then shopping centers, and finally enclosed shopping malls. He not only constructed shopping malls, he began to assemble and run them. By the 1990s, the DeBartolo Corporation had spread far beyond Ohio. The company owned almost a hundred malls and its worth had soared over a billion dollars.

The family gravitated toward the west and south. In California, the DeBartolo family purchased the highly successful San Francisco 49ers in 1977. Son Edward operated the team. An effort to purchase professional baseball teams was thwarted because the family also held interests in several racing tracks.

The DeBartolo family fortunes turned to Florida. In the 1970s, Tampa Mayor Dick Greco resigned from office to work full time building malls for the DeBartolos. In the early 1980s, the family donated a generous gift to the University of South Florida in Tampa to endow the DeBartolo Chair in English. Eddie DeBartolo Jr. resides in Tampa where the family operates the DeBartolo Foundation.

Fashions change, and in Florida, new ideas are always literally and figuratively sweeping away the old and erecting new structures and material designs. As development—or over-development—threatened the quality of life in older Florida communities, some began to question the wisdom of growth-at-any-cost. In Sarasota, real estate financier N.J. Oliveri was intrigued by a section of downtown called Towles Court. Built in the 1920s, Towles Court featured modest-but-charming cottages that appealed to winter residents. By the 1970s, the neighborhood was in steep decline. Oliveri gambled that a refurbished Towles Court would appeal to the sensibilities of a new generation of urban residents. He convinced city officials to change the zoning restrictions and allow structures to combine living and retail space in one building. Artists, printmakers, sculptors, and photographers flocked to the community, purchasing the cottages for $75,000. Today, Towles Court is a commercial and aesthetic success story.

Food

The legacy of Italian-American is etched deeply in the railroads and buildings they constructed, but also by the tastes and smells they introduced. Florida became a hothouse for fruits and vegetables. Chefs and mothers also introduced foodstuffs, such as pasta, to Floridians. An April 1937 headline proclaimed, "Tampans Love Their Spaghetti; Consume Two Tons Each Day." The journalist claimed—without evidence—that more pasta was consumed in Tampa than any comparable sized city in the United States. Two macaroni factories helped satisfy local tastes. Italians also discovered new foodstuffs, some which they could never have found or afforded in the old country. For example, the *New York Times* contended that in 1956, no American city consumed more of the expensive spice saffron than Tampa. Spanish and Italian immigrants had popularized the bright orange crocus threads that turns *arroz con pollo* [chicken with rice] and *risotto Milanese* into a beautiful yellow tint.

In the 1940s, Italian cuisine expanded across America as GIs who had spent time in Italy came home with a familiarity for pizza and pasta. In the late 1940s, Orlando was a modest-sized town with few

Colombi's Restaurant, Saint Armand's Key, Sarasota. 1960s.
Credit: Florida State Archives.

immigrants or second-generation ethnics. Here, too, one could find Italian food. Tony's Bar & Grill on Orange Avenue advertised "'true' Italian spaghetti or Chinese Chop Suey." Joe D. Agostino managed La Cantina Italian Restaurant on Cheney Highway, with "chicken la cacciatore" as a house specialty. Diners could also drive on the Orange Blossom Trail and find Don Ciccio's Italian Restaurant. The 1949 Orlando city directory noted La Pizzaria (the city's first) on N. Parramor, joined by Johnny's Pizza Palace a few years later. In the early 1950s, the D'Agostino family opened the popular Villa Nova in Winter Park.

The service industry dominates Florida's economy, generating hundreds of thousands of jobs. In Florida, as in New York and Ohio, Italians plied their trade in the restaurant business. Florida has been especially inviting to entrepreneurs who have introduced new chains and franchises. Tim Curci was working as a manager at Hops Restaurant and Brewery in Florida, when he and a partner decided to begin an upscale seafood chain. They opened the first Bonefish Grill in St. Petersburg in 2000, and signed a partnership with Outback Steakhouse to expand nationally.

The restaurant business demands long hours and risk taking. Enterprising bakers and restaurateurs followed the crowds to Florida. The Scinicariello family illustrates in classical form the forces of push and pull. Neapolitans, the family settled in Stamford, Connecticut, in 1929, where they opened a bakery. In 1950 the family opened a restaurant, John the Baker. When the family moved to North Miami in 1969, they opened Mario the Baker, which quickly gained a following for its garlic rolls. In 2000, Sal Siragusa and Gino Aprile took over the popular eatery. The Scinicariello family has opened a new Mario the Baker in West Palm Beach. Interestingly, when the restaurant opened in 1969 in North Miami, the area along West Dixie Highway was heavily Italian, Polish, and Greek; today, Haitians make up a large percentage of the population. In North Miami Beach on Dixie Highway, Lorenzo's Italian Market has long been a South Florida institution.

Pizza in Florida may seem and sound disingenuous and dissonant to New Yorkers who feel they have propriety over a classic icon purportedly first created by Gennaro Lombardi in 1901. In reality, pizza, *focaccia,* and *schiaciatta* all share similar roots. Such flatbreads are common to many cultures, and these products evolved over thousands of years to provide workers savory sustenance. Cooked on fire-heated tiles, the wheat flatbreads were sprinkled with cheese, pepper flakes, or garlic to make a quick meal. Tomatoes, of course, did not arrive until the sixteenth century. Mozzarella, the now ubiquitous cheese, dates to antiquity.

When did pizza arrive in Florida? When Sicilian immigrants settled in Tampa in the 1890s, they often built bee-hive ovens called in dialect *furni.* The brick and tile-lined ovens had multiple purposes. The ovens permitted baking to be done outside, thus diminishing the possibilities of fire and keeping kitchens and homes cooler. Most importantly, the ovens produced much-desired breads and pastries. Tampa Italians also opened up a number of prominent bakeries, most notably Alessi's, which began on Cherry Street in West Tampa in 1912, and still operates today. The many Italian-operated dairies furnished cheese and cream. Tampa Italians have been eating fresh mozzarella—a relatively simple cheese to produce—for over a century. Only recently have they put mozzarella on baked flatbread.

Until the 1960s, pizza was a rarity, even in Tampa. Alessi's and other bakeries sold a similar flatbread, *schiaciatta.* Today, pizza may be the most popular food in Florida. Electronic searches list over three thousand establishments advertising pizza—including Pizza Dude in Port Orange—and that figure does not include separate chain locations.

Southeast Florida, the home of hundreds of thousands of transplanted New Yorkers and metropolitans, is now home to dozens of emporiums that advertise "coal-fired pizza," just like that dish first served in Greenwich Village over a century ago. Some even boast authentic Neapolitan San Marzano tomatoes. In Palm Beach County alone, aficionados can patronize Anthony's Coal Fired Pizza, Red Rock Coal Fired Pizza, Coal Mine Pizza (utilizing anthracite coal from Reading, PA), and Fire Rock Pizza. Collier County in Southwest Florida also considers itself a pizza magnet. A 2008 survey by the *Naples Daily News* crowned Aldo's Pizza as tops, followed by Aurelio's.

When asked why he robbed banks, Willie Sutton replied famously, "Because that's where the money is!" It's also one of the reasons why so many famous chefs have sought fame and fortune in South Florida. Nino Pernetti was born in the village of Campione in post-war Italy. His love of cooking has taken him to restaurants in Afghanistan, Korea, Zambia, the Bahamas, Venezuela, and finally Miami. In 1985, he opened Caffé Baci on Ponce De Leon Boulevard, a fabulously successful restaurant.

A Café Baci also exists in Sarasota. The Mei family first established a successful restaurant in Rome, then in New York, and in 1991 opened Café Baci in Sarasota.

Considering the shelf life of most restaurants, operating an establishment for three decades is an accomplishment. Mama Gilda, opened in 1949 in West Plam Beach, was a legendary eatery. Gilda Cioffi, the restaurant's namesake, was the matriarch. A native of Capri, she left Italy in 1929. Her family operated a number of successful restaurants in New York and South Florida. In Tampa, the Iavarone family has operated restaurants for three generations. Malio's on Dale Mabry Boulevard was the Iavarone flagship, a place frequented by mayors, athletes, and celebrities. Closed in 2005, Malio's has been reinvented in 2007 at the a new location.

The Clemente family of Bari, Italy, earned a legendary reputation for their Central Bakery in Union City, New Jersey. Several family members migrated to St. Pete Beach where they have duplicated their talents. La Casa del Pane, in the shadows of the picturesque Hotel Don Cesar, has a loyal following of patrons that appreciate the bakers' *sfogliattele* and freshly-baked breads.

One of Pensacola's most famous restaurants is Joe Patti Seafood. The establishment dates from 1931, when Sicilian-born Captain Joe Patti and his wife Anna began selling seafood from the family back porch. In 1935, they opened Joe Patti's Fish Market. Hurricane Ivan, in 2004, devastated the establishment. In a sensational scandal, restaurant proprietor and prominent Pensacola businessman Frank Patti was sentenced to prison in 2005 for income tax evasion.

Scotto's was the prototypical Italian-American restaurant. Located in Pensacola's Seville Square, an historic district of eighteenth- and nineteenth-century homes and structures, Scotto's Ristorante Italiano evolved from the family's deep association with food, such as the Premier Bakery, which opened in 1945. Sadly, Scotto's could not survive past the millennium, a fate associated with old and new eateries. Symbolically, Dharma Blue, a café, occupies the space today.

If Scotto's represented the classic Italian-American dining establishment, Seaside's Modica Market represents the newest culinary wave. Pensacola's origins date from the 1550s; Seaside originated in the 1980s. But Seaside's influence is enormous. Considered the mother church of "New Urbanism," Seaside's strict building code (dictating wooden siding, metal roofs, and front porches) is widely immitated. Seaside has been so enormously successful that it exists as one of the most upscale communities in America.

In the Seaside town square sits a popular establishment, Modica Market. The path from Sicily to Alabama to North Florida was unlikely. Two families left the Sicilian town of Castellermini at the turn of the twentieth century.

Gaetano D'Alessandro and his bride, Carmela Scozzari, settled briefly in Paterson, New Jersey, before settling in Birmingham, Alabama. They soon opened a popular grocery store in Bessemer, Alabama. The grocery catered to Whites and Blacks who worked in the nearby mills. in spite of fires and depressions, the store survived.

The Modica family left Sicily and immigrated to Richmond, Virginia. The Modicas kept close contact with their Sicilian-Southern *paesani* in Alabama.

in 1946, Charles Modica—the family wanted to name their son Calogero but settled on Charles—joined the armed services and was stationed in Pensacola, Florida. He promised his parents that he would pay a courtesy visit to the D'Alessandro clan, and finally called upon the family in 1948. He hitchhiked from Pensacola to Brimingham, than took the streetcar to Bessemer, which let him off in front of the G&D grocery. He was lovestruck at a young lady behind the counter, Sara Veronica D'Alessandro. They were married in 1949.

Charles Modica went to work for his father-in-law's grocery. The young couple vacationed frequently in Panama City Beach. Following several efforts to buy property and build a small motel, the Modicas stopped along a deserted strip of beach in Walton County. They heard about a new community begun by Robert Davis called Seaside. At this time in the early 1980s, one structure had been built. The Modicas purchased a lot on Tupelo Street then later built a modest home. Founder Robert Davis eventually persuaded the Modicas to open and operate a "gourmet" grocery. In 1989, Modica Market became part of Seaside.

The distinction of having the longest running Italian establishment in Florida goes easily to Castellano & Pizzo. Pietro Pizzolato left Sicily in the 1870s, settling first in New Orleans and then in New Mexico, as foreman of a gold-smelting plant. He invested his savings in Tampa, opening a grocery store. The Castellano & Pizzo store stood on the corner of Eighth Avenue and 18th Street in Ybor City for almost a hundred years. For decades, the establishment made fresh mozzarella, at a time when pizza was unknown to most Floridians. In the 1980s, proprietor Nelson Castellano relocated the store to a more upscale location, where it has thrived.

In 2005, the Podini family, owners of a popular grocery chain in Italy, opened their first store in America. Palladio Italian Gourmet Market opened its first store in Boca Raton in 2006, the first of several in South Florida. Where once Italian mothers spent hours preparing evening meals, today's Italian-American women typically work. Thus, Daniele Podini seized the opportunity to offer customers chef-prepared take-out meals.

Popular cafes and eateries follow the crowds from the Northeast to the Southeast. The popularity of food shows and culinary magazines has made once regional and local foods national crazes. Witness the export of Buffalo wings, Chicago's Vienna-style hot dogs, and Italian beef sandwiches, ethnic delicacies now easily available in the Sunshine State. Until recently, if a gourmand wished to sample Philadelphia cheese steaks, one stood in line at Pat's or Geno's. So commonplace today is the Philly cheese steak that a columnist once proposed outlawing menu items that originated outside their area code.

In Dunedin, a Gulf Coast community that glorifies all things Scottish, one finds LaSpada's. The proprietors take the challenge of replicating Philadelphia cheese steaks so seriously that they import the signature rolls from Amoroso Bakery in the City of Brotherly Love. Potato chips are also available for *i cognoscenti*.

Boca Raton has attracted large numbers of affluent ethnics. S i n c e 1991, from her Boca Raton home, RoseMarie Boniello edits *Preserving*

Our Italian Heritage, a collection of old-world recipes donated by South Florida transplants.

Mazzaro's Italian Market in St. Petersburg typifies the fruits of hard work and location. In the 1990s, Pittsburghers Sam and Pat Cuccaro opened the store, originally as a coffee roasting establishment. It has expanded into one of the finest Italian markets and bakeries, with display cases loaded with cheeses, wine, and baked goods. If one wishes to take the ethnic pulse beat of Florida, stand in line at Mazzaro's on Christmas Eve. Long lines form as customers pick up brick-baked breads and *salsiccia.* If one listens to the accents, many transplanted Italian Americans—but also Eastern and Central European Americans—have found an ethnic oasis.

The ethnic establishment with the most intriguing name belongs to the A&N Italian Pork Store and Deli in Clearwater. Owner Nancy Brown was born Nunziata Pisani in Contursi, Italy, but most customers call her "Mamma." She immigrated to New York in 1967 and moved to Florida in 1981. As a child in Italy, she learned the artisinal craft of curing meats, and A&N features on-the-premises-made *sopresetta* and salami. Other intriguingly named establishments include Two Brothers Pizzeria and Italian Cusine in Bonita Springs. Until the 1980s a sparsely settled crossroads on US 41, Bonita Springs has witnessed a huge increase in population and wealth. Sam Zinzi and Bob Lanzeri (not brothers!) migrated to Lee County to run the highly regarded restaurant. On St. Joseph's Day, they cook dishes using fresh-caught sardines.

Twenty years ago genuine *gelato* was the luxury of Euorpean tourists. While one can purchase the Italian delicacy in frozen food departments, the authentic taste is now widely available at specialty stores. In 2006, the Gelato Company opened in Gainesville. Italian ices, made famous in Astoria, Queens, can be sampled in Florida. Rita's Water Ice Company has opened several franchises in Jacksonville since it opened the first store at Jacksonville Beach in 1993. In Naples, Amalfi Italian Ice offers homesick New Yorkers, Philadelphians, and Bostonians the closest thing to *granitá,* water ice, or Italian slush. Paciugo, a fourth-generation Italian-owned *gelateria,* has opened four stores in Hollywood, Boca Raton, Miami, and St. Petersburg. Another popular chain, Dolce Vita Gelato Café, operates stores in Hollywood, Miami, and Miami Beach. On the "Chowhound" Blog, one can find hundreds of enthusiastic devotees of *gelato*, each recommending their favorite flavors and parlors: Piu Bella on Lincoln Road in Miami Beach, Roma Organic Gelato in Miami, Bacio in City Place in West Palm Beach, Gelateria Del Duomo in Tampa, Il Gelatone in Orlando, and Funari's Italian Creamery in Jacksonville. Boca Raton ranks as Florida's *gelato* capital: Sonny's, Gelato Shoppe Petrini, and Gelato Amore top the list.

Sports celebrities frequently invest in restaurants as a way to connect with fans. Dan Marino operates a number of chic establishments. One of Marino's favorite Miami Dolphins' receivers was Jimmy Cefalo. Today, Cefalo's wine bar is a famous watering hole in Coconut Grove. El Cap's in St. Petersburg is the antithesis of the modern sports bar. Its genesis dates to 1963, although it had been a corner tavern on Fourth Street for decades before that. In 1963, major league baseball umpire and St. Petersburg resident Augie Donatelli informed his half-brother Steve Bonfili of a business opportunity. Bonfili and his wife Rose sold their bar and grill in Pennsylvania and moved to Florida where they operated El Cap for four decades. Donatelli died in St. Petersburg in 1990 and Bonfili passed away in 2008.

In modern America, chefs and cooks have become media celebrities. They, too, have followed the crowd to Florida. In the late 1990s, Marcella Polini Hazan, Victor Hazan, and their son Giuliano, moved to Longboat Key. Hazan, the prima donna of Italian chefs and the author of *More Classic Italian Cooking* (1986) and *Marcella's Italian Kitchen* (1986), teaches culinary classes and writes cookbooks from her homes in Venice, Italy, and Sarasota, Florida. Giuliano, a rising star in culinary circles, also writes cookbooks and teaches cooking at the local Casa Italia.

Decades before the family Hazan became Sarasota celebrities, Sal Cuomo and Sebastian Carbone had introduced Italian food to generations of Sarasotans. Born Severio Cuomo in 1916 in the Bronx, "Sal" fought in World War II and moved to Florida in 1947. He opened and operated Sal's Italian Restaurant and Pizza King of Sarasota. He is credited with bringing pizza to the area. He died in 1992. Sebastian "Steve" Carbone was also born in New York and migrated to Sarasota in 1949. He operated the popular Papa Nick's Restaurant for twenty-five years. He died in 1978. Rose's Pizzaria opened in 1949.

The Naples area has been an especially attractive place to follow waves of Italian retirees and open Italian eateries. In 2006, one could dine like Neapolitans at Asti, Bellagio, Bravo Gianni, Geraci's, Ristorante Ciao, Naples Tomato, Il Fresco, TreAmici, Vesuvio, and Frascati's.

Since the opening of Walt Disney World in 1971, Orlando has evolved from a modestly important crossroads town to one of the most influential cities in the world. Annually, forty-five million tourists and visitors descend upon Central Florida to pay homage to the Disney Empire. Historically, Orlando attracted few Italian immigrants. But the lure of wealth and fame has attracted many Italians who saw opportunities in the food and service industry. In 2006, the $800 million Palazzo del Lago, a 1,260 luxury hotel-condominium development, opened near Disney World on Lake Bryan.

Bergamo's Italian Restaurant is pure 1990s Orlando. Italian food is secondary to the entertainment. Waiters sing opera as well as other popular songs. In 1984, veteran chef Chris Christini opened Christini's in Orlando, a popular establishment. In Maitland, a city near Orlando, the Gentile family operates the popular establishment, Antonio's La Fiamma. In 2005, the popular Italian trattoria, Toastissimo, begun by Franco Cesari, opened its first American location at the Lincoln Plaza in downtown Orlando.

Surely the most unlikely place in Florida to find an Italian general store with deep roots is Melrose, a small hamlet east of Gainesville. Melrose is the home to Chiappini's, a legendary establishment. Begun in 1935 when Giuseppe Chiappini sought his fortune in the nursery business, the store began improbably. A client paid Giuseppe with a lot in the center of the village of Melrose. He then built a general store and persuaded Gulf Oil to install gas pumps. University of Florida author Jim Twitchell has written of the place, "When you pass it, you think redneck. But it's not. It's all about community."

In the ethnic-blending world of the twenty-first century, one should not be surprised to know that the renowned baker at the most famous Jewish delicatesssen, Flakowitz's of Boynton Beach, is Angelo Priozzi. Or that one of the Florida's leading religious figures is Rabbi Barbara Aiello. Her father, Rabbi Antonio Aiello, played trumpet in the Italian Lodge band in Pittsburgh. Barbara spent time as a student rabbi in Fort Lauderdale, has served as spiritual leader at Temple Beth El in Bradenton, and is the only woman reform rabbi in Italy. She lectures on topics such as Jewish roots in Calabria.

In 2008, Emanuele Viscuso received the prestigious Ettore Pepe Award of the Italian Academy of Cuisine. The son of an Italian sculptor and an Italian jazz musician mother, Emanuele was born in Palermo, Sicily, in 1952. Critics have praised his sculptures, his musical compositions, and his acting. He also represents Florida as delegate of the Accademia Italiana della Cucina. He is credited for having "introduced" Italian cuisine to astronauts aboard the International Space Station. Since 2006, he has organized the Sicilian Movie Festival in Miami Beach, where he now resides.

Agriculture

Historically, Italian emigrants fled the fields of Calabria and Campania, eager to exchange the plight of the *contadino* for a future as a factory laborer in Detroit or Paterson. In spite of the efforts of health reformers and civic officials to move Italians from the congested quarters of the Lower East Side to the agriculture fields of the Deep South, few followed. But most Italians accepted the security of an urban future to the insecurities of a rural future. Some came to the South willingly; others came unwillingly. The history of Sicilian cane cutters and day laborers in Mississippi is largely forgotten and lost. A few did manage to discover Sunshine State groves and ranches and found farm labor preferable to factory work. And some managed to succeed wildly, shaping the course of Florida agriculture.

Born in Cincinnati, Ohio, the son of Italian immigrants, Lawrence Gentile went to work early in his father's fruit business. In 1903, he moved to Florida, settling in Orlando in 1906. The Gentile brothers quickly achieved success as growers, packers, and shippers of citrus. In the 1920s, the Gentile firm was the largest single enterprise engaged in the cultivation of citrus in Orange County. In 1956, the giant corporation Minute Maid purchased several thousand acres from the Gentiles for $3 million.

Philip Caruso's life history seems more suited for the dime novel than business page. At age eleven, he accompanied his family from Italy to Ellis Island, and then to Troy, New York. The Caruso family achieved a modicum of success selling fruit from a pushcart and then corner stand. With his father's death, young Caruso became responsible for his family. Moving his family to Peekskill, Philip prospered as a fruit broker.

Told by his doctor that the harsh New York winters would consume him, Caruso moved his family and business to Central Florida. In 1926, he founded Southern Fruit Distributors, Inc. He also began using the Bluebird label exclusively to advertise his product, a move that was wildly successful. He was a pioneer in the canning of juice, building a large canning factory in Winter Garden. He moved his growing operations to Orlando in 1941, erecting laboratories, mills, and plants. Philip Caruso died in 1966, not before he was inducted into the Mid-Florida Business Hall of Fame.

The Caruso family (more than 100 descendents) expanded and extended the empire after the founder's death. At one time, the family owned 6,000 acres of Central Florida. The Carusos leveraged their landholdings to become major developers. In 1998, the last of the family's citrus groves were bulldozed for Horizon West, a housing project.

Some Italian families have moved their agricultural operations to Florida after achieving success elsewhere. Paul J. DiMare has earned the title of "Mr. Tomato" for his success in growing the New World fruit/vegetable once believed poisonous. The DiMare family has been farming in Florida for three generations and today grows tomatoes and other crops in Homestead and Florida City. Buffeted by foreign competition, fuel costs, and labor woes, DiMare told the *Miami Herald* in 2008, "I don't know if there will be a fourth generation in our industry."

In the 1920s, Jerry Chicone Sr. moved from New Jersey to Orange County, Florida. He became a shrewd investor, beginning as a real estate broker in Winter Garden. He ultimately purchased considerable citrus acreage and downtown Orlando properties, selling fruits nd vegetables to survive the hard times. Late in his life, Chicone downplayed his reputation as a savvy businessman, confessing that he had also sold "a lot of acreage" for $2 an acre because it was swampy and isolated. The swampland became Walt Disney World. Chicone also earned a reputation as a philanthropist, contributing to the growth of Valencia Community College and the University of Central Florida.

In Naples, Italy, as well as Naples, Florida, the American cowboy ["il vaccaro"] came of age in the twentieth century on the silver screen.

In Céfalu's Cinema Paradiso as well as New York City's Rialto and Para-
mount, young Italians dreamt of becoming real cowboys. In Florida,
Italians became, in the local vernacular, cow hunters.

In 1945, tens of thousands of Italian Americans, thankful that they
had survived combat, dreamt of a factory job. Al Bellotto dreamt of
returning to his Florida cattle ranch. His father Giovanni, a cheese maker,
had left the Italian Alps for the coal mines of Pennsylvania. The coal
mines took a toll on Giovanni's lungs, and doctors advised him to move
to a sunny climate. He purchased a small farm and some cattle in Lake
City, a small town in North Florida. There he met Annie Waters, a young
woman who was part Seminole and Cherokee. Giovanni then purchased
grove and ranch land in Polk County. In 1925, Al was born at Dundee.

Polk County, equidistant between the Atlantic Ocean and Gulf
Coast, was the fruitbelt of Florida. Italians were not accepted easily
into this society. "When I started grammar school," Al recalled, "foreigners were not accepted. It was nothing to get into a fight three to
four times a day." His father was old world, "tough and hard. He
instilled in us that we had to work hard to get what we wanted in life."
Al excelled at football at Haines City High and then at age seventeen,
volunteered for the navy where he served as a gunner on the *USS York*.
He returned to Polk County and with his new bride and savings accu-
mulated from service, began building the Circle B ranch. From 80
acres, his spread grew to 4,800 acres. He sold for $7.4 million most of
his ranch around Lake Hancock, with the understanding that the land
be preserved as a wildlife refuge. He was recently elected to the Florida
Agricultural Hall of Fame and served as the president of the Florida
Cattleman's Association.

Allison Repetto is the self-described "last of the Mohicans." The
owner of the last commercial orange grove in Pinellas County, Repetto
has become a symbol of a changing Florida. A reporter described him
in a 2004 feature story:

> The last of his kind, Al Repetto limps among his Temple and his navel
> oranges, looking at them, examining leaves, happy at the health of this
> tree, scowling at the brown leaves of another, wondering what the future
> might bring. He will be 80 soon. He was born in Pinellas when citrus was

king, when there seemed to be groves on every block and along every dirt road, when the crisp winter air was perfumed by orange trees in delectable blossom."

In 1946, Repetto returned home to Pinellas County after serving in World War II. He and his brother-in-law purchased a forlorn-looking grove in Largo, renaming it the Orange Blossom Grove. In 2005, Repetto reluctantly decided to retire and sell the groves. He is now a very wealthy man.

The Basore family has been farming in America for three generations in Ohio, Michigan, and, since 1969, in Florida. The family purchased a large tract of land in Belle Glade, a legendary farming community on the southwestern shore of Lake Okeechobee. Belle Glade is the setting in Zora Neale Hurston's searing novel about migrant workers, *Their Eyes Were Watching God.* The Basores, however, have invested heavily in technology. The Basore operations, TKM Farms, is the largest lettuce grower east of the Mississippi, dedicating about 2,000 acres for that specialty winter crop. "If you've eaten in a fast-food restaurant this winter, or any restaurant, you have probably eaten our lettuce," said Toby Basore, in a 2004 interview.

Italian immigrants established several major dairies in Hillsborough County. The Guagliardo, Buggica, Ferlita, Reina, Spoto, and Zambito families adapted their old-world shepherding skills and created dairies that lasted several generations. The Guagliardo dairy that began with a few goats and milk cows evolved into the Florida Dairy.

Florida's Gold Coast and Glitterati

Florida's "Gold Coast," the southeastern part of the peninsula became irresistible to many Americans. The population surge is striking: Consider that in 1950, the combined populations of Dade, Broward, and Palm Beach counties accounted for about 700,000 residents. A half century later, over 3 million inhabitants call the Gold Coast home, and many more come as seasonal residents and tourists.

The vast majority of the new residents pouring into the Gold Coast chose the burgeoning suburbs. New towns, such as Miramar, Golf Village and Coral Springs, and old towns with agricultural pasts, such as Dania, Davie, and Pompano Beach, exploded. Hundreds of thousands of children and grandchildren of Eastern and Southern European immigrants pursued the newest wrinkle of the American Dream.

Many of the new arrivals might have come to Miami or Miami Beach as Army Air Corps trainees in 1943 or as tourists in the 1950s. Miami was simply irresistible. The lush foliage and tropical climate appealed to an America interested in leisure and consumption. The Miami Beach nightclub defined elegance in the post-war years. Tony Bennett (Anthony Benedetto), Dean Martin (Dino Crocetti), Frank Sinatra, Frankie Laine (Frank Lo Vecchio), Julius LaRosa, Jerry Vale, Al Martino, Vic Damone, Bobby Darin (Walden Cassotto) defined style and class at the Hotel Fontainbleau and Eden Roc, Ciro's and the Paddock Club.

Since the 1920s, Jews had developed a love affair with Miami Beach. By the 1940s, Miami Beach had a Jewish mayor and had banned anti-Semitic ordinances. In the film *Godfather II*, Michael Corleone pays a 1950s visit to the aging Jewish mobster Hyman Roth. In real life, Meyer Lansky and Tampa's Santo Trafficante had significant investments and power in Miami Beach—and in the nearby Havana casinos. By the 1970s, most of the affluent Jews had fled to North Miami Beach or Broward or Palm Beach Counties. South Beach was home to a large number of poor and elderly Jews and a crumbling collection of buildings that few people cared about. The renaissance of South Beach marks one of the great architectural preservation moments in Florida and American history. By the late 1980s, Miami Beach's Art Deco hotels, with their streamlined Italianate-designs had become the rage.

California architect Robert Venturi was one of the first to argue for the district's preservation.

Celebrities

In 1984, the television show *Miami Vice* premiered. The show not only attracted millions of viewers, *Miami Vice* helped refurbish Miami's reputation, popularized South Beach, and introduced sun-splashed colors to the young and hip. Impresario Gianni Versace helped design the dazzling pastels worn by Crockett and Tubbs.

In a cruel twist of life imitating art, Versace fell in love with Miami Beach, purchasing for $3 million the historic Casa Casuarina House on Ocean Drive. In a sensational event that seemed like an episode of *Miami Vice*, Versace was killed outside his mansion in 1997. But Versace had helped make Miami Beach a gilded playground for the stars. Italian-American celebrities Madonna and Sylvester Stallone call Miami Beach home. Star watchers who miss the real Madonna can attend Jennifer Follia's impersonation of Madonna at numerous South Beach night clubs. Diners wishing to spot celebrities flock to Robert De Niro's sushi palace on Collins Avenue.

Not all Italian-American celebrities sought the glitz of South Beach and Ocean Drive. Perry Como, the son of Abruzzi immigrants and the singing barber from Canonsburg, Pennsylvania, spent his golden years at Jupiter, Florida. Como never forgot his roots, but enjoyed the solitude of his Martin County enclave, ranked as one of America's most exclusive places. John Travolta, perhaps the most glamorous of the glitterati, maintains a Florida home at Jumbolair, a gated community near Ocala featuring a private runway for its jet-set residents.

Diva Norma Tina Russo was a native of New York City that came to Tampa in 1932. She became one of the grand figures of Italian opera in Florida. In 1954, she helped found the Tampa Grand Opera Association.

Exemplifying the diversity of the state's Italian-American experience, Judy Canova was a Floridian. Born in 1913 in the northeast Florida community of Starke, the daughter of a cotton-broker father and sing-song mother, Judy claimed ancestral links to the famed Italian sculptor Antonio Canova. Classically trained, she earned a reputation as a wide-eyed, banjo-playing, corn-pone performer, a more beautiful version of Minnie Pearl. Her career rocketed after appearing on the Rudy Valle radio show. During World War II she toured in the USO while hosting "The Judy Canova Show," and later starred in several movies. In 1946, she built an ocean-front home in New Smyrna, Volusia County. Upon her death in 1983, the yodeling, pig-tail-coiffed actress and comedian was eulogized as "the queen of the hillbillies."

In the 1950s and 1960s, no single group mustered more swagger or prestige than the men with the "right stuff," America's astronauts. Walter "Wally" M. Schirra was born in New Jersey, was graduated from the US Naval Academy in 1945, attended pilot training at the Pensacola Naval Air Station, and will always be known as one of the original seven astronauts, and the only one to have flown on all three aircraft: Mercury, Gemini, and Apollo. Schirra, the fifth American in space, died in May 2007.

The first Italian-American female astronaut was Lisa Caputo Nowak. After receiving her commission from the US Naval Academy in 1985, she compiled a distinguished flight record. In 1996, she was selected by NASA and qualified as a mission specialist. In July 2006, she became a celebrated astronaut by virtue of her thirteen-day flight in the Space Shuttle Discovery; in February 2007, Nowak became a different type of celebrity when she drove from Houston to Orlando for the purpose of confronting and accosting a rival astronaut. She was arrested amid a bizarre media avalanche.

Tony Signorini, too, deserves his 15 minutes of fame. Reunited with his wife Elsie after the war, the couple visited Clearwater in December 1945 to see her parents. He asked simply, "Do you want to go back?" So the Signorinis became residents of Clearwater. The former Pennsylvanian found a job at an electrical appliance store. One day Tony was reading a *National Geographic* with photographs of dinosaur tracks. He gleefully showed the photograph to his boss, who was a practical joker. They went to work and fashioned monster dinosaur feet. Into the mold they poured lead and fastened the scary-looking contraption to high-topped gym shoes. Each foot-claw weighed thirty pounds. Tony, an air force veteran, explained the next move in an interview sixty years after the event:

Al and I rowed out to the beach. I put on the shoes. I jumped out of the boat in shallow water. I was young then, about 25 or so, and much stronger than I am now, an old man. I had to kind of swing my legs out to the side and then forward to get going. Somehow I didn't break my legs. I left deep tracks about six feet apart. I made this big loop from the surf, up the beach, and then back into the water to the boat.

Newspapers declared that a "Clearwater Monster" had prowled the beach. For nearly sixty years, no one except his wife realized that Tony Signorini was the "Clearwater Monster." In June 2006, *St. Petersburg Times* writer Jeff Klinkenberg's exposé revealed the source of those mysterious dinosaur tracks.

Arturo Mennillo was one of Florida's greatest photographers. He took photographs in Africa, Asia, and Europe, but his heart always remained in his native Northwest Florida. His family tree included branches in Italy but also the Deep South. Arturo was especially fond of the Fort Walton Beach-Destin area, where he began taking his first photographs at local football games and fish camps. He left the area in 1966 to document the war in Southeast Asia. He returned to capture on film a vanishing, pristine Florida. He died in 1996, but his legacy lives on in thousands of negatives and books such as *Highway to Heaven* (1998).

Italian-American youth participated in one of modern America's rites-of-passage. In 1961, Fort Lauderdale was a sleepy beach town, the spring home to the New York Yankees. But spring, itself, was changing. John F. Kennedy was president and youth would be served. On 21 December 1960, Fort Lauderdale's Gateway Theatre was the site for the world premier of *Where the Boys Are.* A song of the same name became a monster hit, catapulting Connie Francis (formerly Concetta Franconero) to stardom. Four months later, 50,000 college students poured into Broward County to experience "Spring Break." Newspaper reports and police files document the presence of Victor Galline, a University of Wisconsin student, who was charged with throwing a live, six-foot hammerhead shark into a motel swimming pool. Interestingly, Fort Lauderdale policeman Lt. George Franza and Chief of Police Joe Iacono, are indelibly etched in Spring Break lore. An exasperated Iacono told reporters, "This area is full of oldsters who

visit here for rest and quiet and I'm not going to let a few hoodlums dis-
turb their rest and endanger their lives."

Designer Angelo Donghia moved from New York City to Key West
in the 1970s when America's southernmost city was forlorn and seedy.
He had achieved success as a businessman and designer, owning Vice
Veers fabric house and Burghe-Donghia Interiors, but he was determined to restore Key West. In 1974, he purchased his first home in Key
West's Old Town district, spending $200,000 in refurbishing the struc-
ture. He fell in love with a "Key West raunchiness" that was "visually
appealing" and "cosmopolitan." The city's tolerance made the Keys a
very attractive place for gays and lesbians. The Angelo Donghia Foundation, based in New York, awards scholarships to students of interior
design. Italian designer Donatella Linari resides in Fort Lauderdale.

Eastern and Southern European immigrants brought their musical
traditions with them, and at the center of working-class popular culture was the accordion. The accordion was everywhere. Alfonso
LaRocca typified the men and women who played the lively accordion.
Al LaRocca and his Serenades Band were an institution at the Italian
Club and Sons of Italy Hall in Tampa, but also German beer gardens
and Polish weddings. He was playing until his 89th year, when he
passed away in 2006.

Italian Americans shaped the artistic and musical experiences in
Florida. Tampa's L'Unione Italiana erected a theater, where touring
operas played in the first decades of the twentieth century. In 1919, for
instance, playbills advertised that Madame Mimi Aguglia was performing "the tragic role of Francesca di Rimi."

The rich musical traditions inspired young Italian Americans to
enter the theater and stage. A famous diva lived in Tampa: Norma Tina
Russo, born in Naples, trained in Italy, and came to the US on a concert
tour in the 1920s. She moved to Tampa in 1932 and became actively
involved in the musical scene.

Under the Big Top

As the capital of illusion, Florida was also home to circuses, carni-
vals, and a retinue of stars and performers: acrobats, tightrope walk-
ers, jugglers, lion tamers, and equestrians. Italians figured mightily.

Much was expected of Bobby Berosini. Nine generations of animal trainers preceded him. The family had left Italy several generations earlier and settled in Czechoslovakia. "When the communists came to power," he explained in 1977, "they took the circus and left Papa Berosini with seven children to feed. My father did not have animals to train, but he had us kids, so he trained us. We became a Risley act— two acrobats that juggle objects or people with their legs." The family defected in 1959 to the United States, settling in Gibsonton, Florida, the Gulf Coast winter home of circus performers. The Berosinis returned to their first love—animal training. Bobby was one of Busch Gardens early performers and trainers.

The Zacchini family defined the glamour and danger of the modern circus. The Zacchinis performed around the world but called Tampa home since the 1930s. In 1922, while performing in Cairo, Egypt, family patriarch Edmondo Zachini attempted a feat that would electrify audiences. He wondered whether a human being could survive being shot from a cannon. Powered by a crude, spring-powered cannon, he was hurled twenty feet through the air. Unfortunately, the fall broke his leg, but through adjustments and the installation of a safety net, he perfected the technique of a "human bullet" soaring over 100 feet.

Edmondo's large family of six brothers, two sisters, and many children burnished the Zacchini name. Gradually, the idea of a female human cannonball materialized. In 1938, Josephine Zacchini edged toward history by becoming the first woman to pull the trigger of the cannon.

World War II provided the perfect opportunity. Even "human cannonballs" were in short supply. Egle and Duina, the daughters of Edmondo "the Great Zacchini," volunteered. In 1943, while on a USO tour, Egle, aka "Miss Victory"—adorned in a white leather jump suit with red and blue ribbons—hurtled at 100 mph through the air. Altogether, eleven separate Zacchinis became human cannonballs, from Brunhilde to Vittorio. By 1972, the Zacchini cannons were silent. A combination of serious injuries and jaded audiences made human cannonballs obsolete.

Sarasota, home of John Ringling and the winter headquarters for the most famous circuses in the world, was also home to myriad Italian performers. In 1934, circus magnate Jon Ringling witnessed a circus performance by an Italian family in Europe. He immediately invited them to Florida. Ernesto Cristiani, the Italian-born patriarch of one of the world's oldest circus families, brought his 15 children to Sarasota. A native of Modena, Italy, *il Circo Cristiani* had been performing in circuses since the early nineteenth century. The Cristianis needed few outsiders, since they tumbled, rode horses bareback, and performed on the tightrope and high rings. Ernesto died in Sarasota in 1973.

Oscar Adolfo Cristiani died in 1989. He had participated in the last Cristiani family performance in 1965. Belmonte Cristiani remembered his brother, "Not only was Oscar an expert bareback rider, he was a great trainer of all animals. He could train any animal from horses to elephants."

In 1958, the last circus left Sarasota. Some stars remained in town; others left. At his death in South Miami in 1973, Con Colleano was eulogized as the "greatest tight-wire walker that ever lived." A native Australian, Colleano was the first person to perform a forward somersault on the high wire. He first worked in the circus as a clown at age four. He retired to Miami in 1960.

Genovaffa "Mamma" Canestrelli was born in Brindisi, Italy, in 1902. She became a cinema star as well as a diva soprano at Naples' San Carlos Opera House. There she met and married the circus equestrian Ottavio Canestrelli. She joined his circus troupe and the family came to America in 1934. They opened Sarasota's first dinner theater, Casa Canestrelli, where "Mamma" cooked and sang during and between circus acts. She later established La Tosca Trailer Park (named after her daughter!) "Mamma" died in Mexico City in 1996.

The biggest circus star of them all was Al Tomaini. Born in New Jersey in 1912, young Al grew and grew until he reached eight feet, four inches. He found his calling as the gentle giant, a circus performer. The giant fell in love with Bernice "Jeanie" Smith, who was two feet, six inches high. They married and moved to Gibsonton, Florida, on the Gulf Coast in 1940. Gibsonton was acquiring a reputation as the winter capital for America's "carnies." Al and Jeanie opened up Giant's Camp Restaurant, a place famous for its enormous biscuits. Al Tomaini died in 1962.

If Italians share an intimacy with the circus, it is also true they are synonymous with fireworks. In South Florida, the Zambelli sisters are a Fourth-of-July tradition. The family business spans three centuries and has performed for presidents and kings.

Writers

Writers and artists have found Key West's isolation and charm irresistible. In the 1930s, Elizabeth Bishop and Ernest Hemingway discovered Key West. John Ciardi, arguably the most accomplished Italian-American man of letters of the twentieth century, also made Key West his home. He lived in a writers' compound near Solares Hill—at 16 feet above sea level, the island's highest land mass. Neighbors included John Hersey and Ralph Ellison.

Born in 1916 Boston, the son of Italian immigrant parents, John Ciardi was raised in Boston's North End and attended New England colleges and the University of Michigan. As a young student, he held strong opinions about the threat of fascism and totalitarianism. Pearl Harbor was a clarion call to duty, but his leftist opinions delayed his assignment. He told Studs Terkel how fate intervened.

> When I came up for graduation from the navigation school, I was classi-fied as a PAF—a premature anti-fascist. I did not get a commission. A year later I heard that all 44 men of my graduating class were either dead or missing in action. When we got to Saipan, I was a gunner on a B-29. It seemed certain to me that we were not going to survive.

Ciardi survived, returning from the war deeply scarred, scared, and grateful. His scholarship and writings between the late 1940s and 1970s are simply stunning. He taught at Harvard, edited the *Saturday Review*, authored numerous books, most notably *How Does a Poem Mean?* (1959), and wrote twenty-one volumes of poems. Biographer Edward Cifelli wrote, "He wrote love poems, too, and poems about his Italian heritage." Ciardi's most monumental achievement was an acclaimed English translation of Dante Alighieri's *Inferno* (1954 ed).

Author Philip Caputo also sought the solitude and solace of Key West. Born in 1941, a native of Chicago, Caputo served in the Marine

Corps in Vietnam, an experience etched in one of his memorable works, *A Rumor of War* (1977), and went to work for the *Chicago Tribune,* where he won the Pulitzer Prize for his investigative journalism.

Before Key West was home to Ciardi and Caputo, it was the residence of Tennessee Williams. In Key West, the tortured but brilliant playwright wrote *The Rose Tattoo,* which received a Tony for best play in 1951. Biographers believe the play was Williams' homage to his sister Rose and his partner, Frank Merlo. The play involves the life of a Sicilian immigrant in Louisiana, Serafina Delle Rose. In the 1955 movie version, Anna Magnani played the sensuous and tempestuous Serafina opposite Burt Lancaster as Alvaro Mangiacavallo. Interestingly, the movie was filmed not in Louisiana, but in Key West's old cigarmaker quarters. The film introduced Magnani, who won best actress in the drama; it was also her first English-speaking movie role. Williams was a gracious host and many friends visited him, including Truman Capote, whose family may have been Italian.

The personal saga of Michael Shaara is as compelling as the subjects he wrote about. The son of an Italian immigrant father/prize fighter who settled in Jersey City, New Jersey—an official at Ellis Island changed the spelling from Sciarra—Michael's path to writing took many turns. He was graduated from Rutgers University in 1951, but before his literary career commenced, he served stints as a paratrooper with the 82nd Airborne, a merchant seaman, and a policeman in St. Petersburg, Florida. He later reflected, "The year on the police force in St. Petersburg taught me more about creative writing than all the courses I had at Rutgers or Columbia. I saw people in crisis. I saw people as they really were." His mother moved to St. Petersburg in 1947, followed by his father five years later.

In 1961, he began teaching English at Florida State University. A prolific author, he wrote scores of essays, short stories, and books, but never experienced the acclaim he sought. In 1965, he suffered a heart attack, the first of many medical setbacks. For over a decade, he was obsessed with the idea of writing a novel about the Civil War battle at Gettysburg. Fifteen publishers rejected his manuscript, until finally in 1973, a small company agreed to publish *Killer Angels.* Critically acclaimed, sales were modest.

Demons continued to haunt Shaara. While teaching in Florence, Italy, he crashed his motorcycle, suffering serious brain damage. It took him years to regain his writing faculties. In 1988, a second heart attack claimed his life. Ironically, *Killer Angels* became a number one bestseller after his death. The adaptation of his novel for the 1993 film *Gettysburg* brought posthumous fame and the reconciliation with his estranged son Jeff, who wrought a prequel and sequel to his father's book. The Michael Shaara papers are housed at the Bienes Center for the Literary Arts in Fort Lauderdale.

Sports

The state of Florida has become a rich source of athletic talent. Just as the diamond, gridiron, and boxing ring once served as an escape for young men destined for Pennsylvania coal mines and steel mills, Florida has become a prime exporter of athletes. Italian Americans, who in the 1930s and 1940s saw baseball as a way out of a working-class life, are now more likely to see a contract as a way to lifetime security. Florida continues to export athletes, but young baseball and football players are more likely Haitian, Cuban, or African American, and come from places like Belle Glades, Liberty City, or Jacksonville.

Few cities in America can rival Tampa's roster of baseball players. Al Lopez, the son of Spanish immigrants, led the way in the 1920s. Ybor City and West Tampa became a baseball hothouse, producing two great baseball managers: Lou Piniella (Spanish) and Tony LaRussa. Middle-class white neighborhoods sent Steve Garvey and Wade Boggs to the major leagues. Dwight Gooden, Gary Sheffield, and Derek Bell emerged from the African-American community.

Since the 1970s, Florida-born, Italian-American baseball players include Kurt Bevacqua (born 1947 in Miami Beach), Jeff D'Amico (born 1975 in St. Petersburg), Lenny DiNardo (born 1979 in Miami), Jeff Fiorentino (born 1983 in Pembroke Pines), Sam Salvatore Militello (born 1969 in Tampa), Rich Montleone (born 1963 in Tampa), Nick Regilio (born 1978 in Miami), and John Romano (born 1979 in Tampa).

The 1971 movie *Brian's Song* forever linked Brian Piccolo with the Chicago Bears. But long before he was blocking for Gayle Sayers, he was a legendary athlete in Fort Lauderdale. Judge William Zloch remembers playing on the same Central Catholic football team in Fort

Lauderdale. "Brian was an underdog, and that drove him." His athletic accomplishments won him a scholarship to Wake Forest University. At Wake Forest, Piccolo led the nation in rushing and scoring. Signed as a free agent with the Bears, Piccolo and Gayle Sayers became the first white and black players to room together on the road. The Brian Piccolo Park Velodrome in Cooper City honors his memory.

Lee Corso is best known as the opinionated analyst for ESPN, but he first gained fame as a five-foot, nine-inch star football player at Miami's Jackson High. In 1953, he enrolled at Florida State University, a school that had been an all-female school until 1947. Corso demonstrated great versatility, playing running back and defensive halfback. His senior year he quarterbacked the Seminoles, leading the team in total yardage, punt returns, and interceptions. His college roommate was a Riviera Beach player named Burt Reynolds. An inductee in the Florida Sports Hall of Fame, the Lake Mary resident coached at the University of Tampa, Louisville, and Indiana.

Fran Curci has also sunk deep roots in the Sunshine State. A quarterback for the University of Miami in the late 1950s, he played briefly for the Dallas Texans of the American Football League. Coaching took him to the University of Miami, University of Tampa, and the University of Kentucky. In 1991 he was hired as head coach of the Tampa Bay Storm, a team in the new Arena Football League. He retired after coaching the team to the league's first championship, He also worked for Westwood One Radio. Curci is a member of the Florida Sports Hall of Fame.

Dick Vitale has lived in Sarasota since the 1990s. The New Jersey native and coach of the Detroit Pistons has become an icon since his debut on ESPN in the early 1980s, and today, he frequently broadcasts from his 13,000 square foot Mediterranean-style home. He is an inductee in the Florida Sports Hall of Fame and is an active fund-raiser for Sarasota charities.

In a media-saturated, sports-crazy world, many professional athletes succumb to the temptations of greed and self-absorption. Such was not the case with Nick Buoniconti. Born in Springfield, Massachusetts, the son of an Italian baker, Buoniconti was an undersized All-American linebacker on a losing team at Notre Dame University. Drafted in the thirteenth round by the Boston Patriots, the 220-pounder became a star and a fan favorite in his native New England. Traded to the Miami Dolphins in 1969, he became the leader of the famed "No Name defense" that achieved an undefeated season in 1972.

After playing fourteen seasons of professional football, Buoniconti accomplished even more off the field. He displayed leadership skills and business acumen, earning a law degree and becoming a corporate leader and a media celebrity for his work on sports shows. But financial success meant little in 1985, when his son Marc suffered paralysis while playing football. He devoted his life to raising money and awareness for this terrible malady. The Buoniconti Fund to Cure Paralysis has raised more than $100 million.

Like his fellow Miami Dolphin, Daniel Constantine Marino has chosen to remain in South Florida after his playing days. A high school legend in western Pennsylvania and an All-American at the University of Pittsburgh, Marino achieved near-instant stardom when he joined the Miami Dolphins in 1983. In seventeen years, Marino broke many hallowed records in the National Football League. In retirement, he has succeeded in a variety of business ventures—most notably Dan Marino's Town Tavern.

When the Jacksonville Jaguars began their NFL debut in 1995, the team selected Tony Boselli as their first draft choice. Boselli, a six-foot-seven-inch, 322-pound offensive tackle, played with such finesse and intensity that he was named to the NFL's All-Decade Team of the 1990s. In 2006, he became the first player to be inducted into the Pride of the Jaguars Place of Honor.

Major league baseball star Mike Piazza attended Miami-Dade Community College but, upon retiring, now resides in Boynton Beach. The list of Italian-American athletes who retired to Florida is long. The sun—and the state's tax breaks—attract the elderly and rich. Golfer Gene Sarazen (born Eugenio Saraceni) died in Naples in 1989, while jockey Eddie Arcaro died in Miami in 1997.

In the late 1950s, the "Raging Bull" Jake LaMotta moved to Miami Beach where he operated a nightclub ay 2100 Collins Avenue. LaMotta's place in Florida will forever be known because of the 1980 film *Raging Bull*, when a corpulent Robert DeNiro depicts LaMotta as having hit rock bottom. The nightclub has been razed and is now the site of a Lum's Restaurant.

Since the 1920s, Italian-American athletes have become so commonplace. Italian-American chief operating officers of sports franchises,
however, are still rare. Vince Naimoli has demonstrated a shrewd business hand in his career. A native of New York City, Naimoli attended
Notre Dame University. Moving to Tampa in 1967, he succeeded in turning around Anchor Glass Company and Harvard Industries. In 1991, he
spearheaded an effort to bring a major league team to the Tampa Bay
area. Ironically, a fellow Italian American was leading another group also
determined to lure a major league team to the region.

Two powerful forces, immigration and the Great Depression,
shaped Frank Morsani's life. Born in Michigan in 1931, Morsani was the
son of Italian immigrants. His father, a welder, moved around the
country in search of work and the American dream. In 1945, his father
purchased a 400-acre farm outside Tulsa, Oklahoma. Young Morsani
appreciated the work ethic demanded by his father. "The farm was pri-
marily my responsibility to take care of. . . . My dad worked away from
the farm six months a year. I got up at 5 a.m. to milk the cows and I'd
get home from school and run the tractor." In his spare time, he shined
shoes, delivered newspapers, and worked at an ice house.

Machinery fascinated young Morsani. Supplementing his income as
a mechanic at local gas stations, he enrolled at Oklahoma A&M
University, majoring in automotive technology. He then enlisted in the
navy, serving in the Korean War. Returning to Oklahoma to finish his
education, Morsani then worked for Ford Motor Co. In the early 1960s,
he moved to Fort Lauderdale to manage a Lincoln-Mercury operation. In
1970, he became general manager of a Mercedes Benz and Toyota deal-
ership in Tampa. The following year, he purchased the company. In the
following decades, he built an automotive empire in Tampa and around
the country. "I didn't ever want to be poor again," he stated. He has been
recognized for his business acumen, but also lauded for his philanthropy
and service. In the late 1980s, he headed a baseball consortium attempting to bring a major league franchise to Tampa. Rebuffed, Morsani sued
Major League Baseball, alleging that his investment group had been
promised a franchise. The media also speculated that the lords of baseball spurned Morsani because of his alleged links to organized crime, a
charge vociferously denied. In 1995, the Vince Naimoli group won an
expansion franchise, the Tampa Bay Devil Rays. After a decade of large-

ly disappointing finishes, lackluster crowds, and criticism of his leadership, Naimoli sold his interest in the team.

Arguably, Nick Bollettieri is one of America's most powerful and influential sports figures. Born in Pelham, New York, in 1931, he is a 1953 graduate of Spring Hill College in Mobile, Alabama. Following military service, he dropped out of the University of Miami Law School to teach tennis. In 1977, he moved to Longboat Key, Florida, to work in the famed Colony Beach and Tennis Resort. In 1978, he opened the Nick Bollettieri Tennis Academy in Bradenton. He is considered a tennis guru by many. Notable alumni of his academy include Andre Agassi, Jimmy Arias, Jennifer Capriati, Monica Seles, Pete Sampras, and Maria Sherapova.

The summer of 2008 introduced many Americans to Rocco Mediate. In a "Rockyesque" storyline, Mediate, whose career had nearly ended because of recurring back pain, emerged from obscurity to nearly defeat Tiger Woods in the US Open. Born in 1962 in Greensburg, Pennsylvania, Mediate attended Florida Southern College in Lakeland before turning professional golfer in 1985. He resides in Naples, Florida, where he is a fixture at the Calusa Pines golf course.

Sadly, the obituary page represents one of the best sources of uncovering remarkable stories about Italian Americans. On September 11, 2008, a *Sarasota Herald-Tribune* headline enticed readers, "World War II Postponed Olympic Gymnast's Dream." The article described the story of Vinnie D'Autorio, who had moved to Sarasota in the 1960s. Here he invested in some successful real estate projects on Siesta Key and owned a seafood restaurant. Born in Newark, New Jersey in 1915, D'Autorio qualified for the US Olympic gymnast team in 1940, but war interrupted his dream. The five-foot-four-inch D'Autorio volunteered for the US Navy and trained aboard ships by erecting makeshift parallel bars and trampolines. When he returned to New Jersey after the war, he coached at Panzer College, launched his own gymnastics school, and competed in the 1948 Olympics in London, England, but failed to win a medal. In 1971, he was inducted into the US Gymnasts Hall of Fame. In 1996, he proudly carried the Olympic torch through the streets of Sarasota.

The Past Is Prologue

The 2000 US Census graphically illustrates the Italian presence in Florida. Over one million residents (out of a total population of 16 million) identified themselves as Italian Americans. Florida, once too distant and unattractive, had become the fourth largest state in the Union and the sixth most important in terms of Italian-American residents. To put this into perspective, Florida has more Italian Americans (1,003,977) than all of the other southern states combined, and ranks comfortably ahead of the states of Illinois, Massachusetts, and Connecticut.

The state of New York has sent the greatest number of transplants southward. Upstate cities such as Utica, Buffalo, and Oswego have been declining for many decades, but the demographics of New York City are especially striking. For a century, Bensonhurst was the largest Italian neighborhood in Brooklyn. But the 2000 census confirmed what lemon ice dealers have known for some time: Italians are leaving the old neighborhoods. The Italian population of Bensonhurst today is half that of two decades ago. As late as 1970, the Italian population of New York was one million; by 2000, it had fallen below 700,000. Some died, some moved to the suburbs, but many have chosen Florida as home. For New York City Jews, the demographic decline has been even more severe. As recently as the late 1950s, New York City's Jewish population stood at 2 million; by 2000, and for the first time since the 1890s, it had plunged below 1 million.

Large numbers of Italian Americans have appeared in a historical blink of an eye where almost none resided a century earlier. One of every thirteen residents of Sarasota, Charlotte, and Manatee counties is Italian American. Thomas Franzone typifies the newest wrinkle of Florida living—and dying. When he was born in 1929, Charlotte County had a population of just 4,013. Franzone, a native of Queens and a Korean War veteran, retired to Port Charlotte in 1988. He was a member of the local Italian American Club.

Broward County is the capital of *italianitá* in twenty-first century Florida. The Miami-Fort Lauderdale metropolitan area is the country's eleventh most populated center for Italian Americans, its 206,119 *paesani* ranking ahead of Providence-Warwick, Rhode Island, Hartford,

Connecticut, and Rochester, New York. Not surprisingly, transplanted ethnics have chosen major metropolitan areas to reside. Of America's fifty metropolitan areas with the most Italian Americans, seven are located in Florida:

#11	Miami-Fort Lauderdale	206,119
#13	Tampa-St. Petersburg	199,457
#27	West Palm Beach-Boca Raton	106,774
#31	Orlando	99,033
#44	Jacksonville	44,953
#46	Daytona Beach	42,719
#47	Sarasota-Bradenton	41,407

Here, too, questions persist. How do residential patterns and new customs in Fort Lauderdale and Deerfield Beach (eating, walking, and gossiping) connect with life in Canarsie and Bensonhurst, Chicago Heights and Elgin? What institutions (permanent and mental) do transplants (young and old) impose on a new place other than rudeness at intersections? Over 150,000 Italian American reside in Broward County's sprawling retirement communities and gated complexes. Palm Beach (106,774), Pinellas (81,833), Hillsborough (63,021), Miami-Dade (52,545), Sarasota (25,082), and Orange (47,701) counties are the most populous. Every county in Florida's sixty-seven constituencies have some Italian Americans; Liberty County, straddling the majestic Apalachicola River and ranked as the state's smallest county, even boasts sixty *paesani*. According to the 2000 census, the counties where the percentage of Italian American residents is highest are Flagler and Hernando counties. Flagler and Hernando are the fastest-growing counties in the state. To put this into perspective, consider that in 1950, the two counties *combined* population was only 10,000 persons.

To paraphrase Hector St. John de Crevecoeur, "What then is this new Floridian?" What is the state of ethnicity in a state of bewildering social and demographic change? In 1971, a *Palm Beach Post* reporter ventured into the Italian-American Club at 624 Nottingham Avenue. She asked many of the same questions, and the members grappled with questions that lie at the heart of the Italian-American experience.

"We've lost a lot," lamented Andrew Busalacchi. "The language is being forgotten. Our children don't even know it. We used to have Italian folk festivals and feasts with native costumes." Harry Cappola added, "And then there was a game we used to play called *bocce*." The club still held an annual ball in honor of Columbus. The 120 members of the Palm Beach Italian-American Club are nearly all gone. Italian language is spoken by even fewer Italian Americans. Most of the children, grandchildren, and great-grandchildren of the immigrant generation have married non-Italians, do not play *bocce*, and seldom attend ethnic festivals. To most Americans who have visited Florida, the most familiar Italian landmark in the Sunshine State in the Italian Pavilion at EPCOT at Walt Disney World, with its copies of Italian masterpieces.

In a 1996 column in the *Florida Times-Union*, a reporter began, "There's no Chinatown in Jacksonville. No Little Italy. No Little Havana. No Korea Town." But Pat Arena, the president of the local Italian-American Club, explained that such ethnic colonies distinguished their parent's generation, not present-day Florida.

Nearly all of the members of the Palm Beach Italian-American Club believed that what identified them as Italians transcended ethnic festivities and rituals or tourist trips to Walt Disney World. Being Italian meant distinctive and meaningful attitudes and obligations toward family and friends, and a special ethos toward work and home. Everything—childhood and death, food and play—must be understood within the context of these special values. The pivotal question remains: When one leaves family and friends in New York or Ohio, what does it mean to be Italian in Florida? Clearly, Florida is a new frontier in the Italian-American experience.

This point is clearly articulated each day on the Italian Americans Discussion Forum, available on ItalianAmericans.com. On the blog, Kim writes, "We recently moved from the Little Italy neighborhood in Niagara Falls, New York to Florida and I was wondering if there might be any Little Italy neighborhoods in Florida?" She added, "I'm homesick for Little Italy to be very honest." Lorena responded with the good news: "Lots of Italians on the east coast (Fort Lauderdale) . . . in and around Tampa . . . buon fortune.'" Daniel suggested that "homesick in Florida" try Clearwater. Still another blogger mentioned that he had a condo at Melbourne Beach. "There are lots of Italians from Michigan, Ohio, New Jersey, and New York. We just had a super fest. The Publix Supermarket sells *mortadella, supresetta, capacola,* and salami, and it's good stuff. They even have Calabrese bread." And finally a new member declared, "There are A LOT of Italians in Naples. There is an Italian American Club."

The case of Venice—Florida, not Italy—is illustrative. Founded originally as a retirement home for members of the Brotherhood of Locomotive Engineers, the city's beginnings were unusual by Florida standards. In 1916, Dr. Fred Albee launched plans for a model city. City planner and architect David Nolan, borrowing from European models, envisioned a city of wide boulevards and parks. Even though Venice never embraced fully Nolan's model, the city is still striking. Huge numbers of Italian Americans call this Sarasota County community home. The Italian American Club of Venice was packed during the 2006 World Cup games. Demographers point out that membership in the Italian American Club has dropped precipitously in the last decade. The city mandates Northern Italian architectural standards, such as terra cotta tile roofs and stucco walls. Betty Intagliata chairs the city's historical commission. Many city streets bear Italian names. The local Dairy Queen took three design revisions to win board approval. The city's newest park, constructed upon a former sewage plant, was christened Tramonto Vista. Since 1988, Venetians have celebrated an Italian Feast and Carnival. In 2005, 40,00 showed up.

Each generation frets that the values and customs that meant so much to them will not survive the next generation. For religious sects as well as immigrant groups, it represents the American jeremiad. Italian immigrants who came to America in great waves before 1920 are gone. Most of their children—the so-called great generation—are gone. Each day, over a thousand World War II veterans die.

What do we make of third-generation Italian Americans who are buying second homes along Florida's coasts and retiring early to Boynton Beach and Marco Island? Unlike their *nonni* or *parenti,* Americans find them, well, very American. A hundred years ago, New England ministers and southern editors pontificated that hordes of Italians were polluting America's racial stock. "Beaten men from beaten races" threatened the social fabric of America. In time, Italians evolved from being dangerous to simply exotic. In the 1920s, Protestants and old stock Americans ventured into Little Italy to see "the other" and dine at an authentic Italian ristorante. In the 1960s, a new generation of young scholars entered graduate school to write "history from the bottom up." Nothing seemed more exotic than the saga and struggle of Italian immigrants. But something happened between the 1970s and the new millennium. In the words of scholar Rudolph Vecoli, "When did Italians become white folks?" New waves of immigrants from Latin America and Asia and the assimilation of European ethnic groups pushed Italians from the bottom rail to mainstream.

Nothing in America is more certain than the death of ethnicity. Unless, of course, it's the rebirth of ethnicity! Precisely at the moment sociologists and journalists eulogize the decline of Italian-American ethnicity, new revivals appear. Fifty years ago, pundits announced that television would erode ethnicity, creating one vast, unaccented, homogenous American culture. But cable has given the electronic hearth new possibilities. Thousands of Floridians subscribe to RAI (Radio Audizione Italia), Italy's public television channel. In July 2006, Italian Americans cheered at hundreds of pubs and sports bars for Italy's victorious World Cup soccer team. At Tampa's Italian Club and other venues, young children are learning Italian. Italian food and Italian chefs are more popular than ever. Molto Mario and Marcella Hazan have become public icons in remote places in Florida. At the 2005 Sarasota Book Festival, large crowds pressed to tell Lidia Bastianich how much they loved her cooking show on public television. Food!

Considering that many current Italian Americans residing in Florida are senior citizens, will their sons and daughters find the Sunshine State an attractive place to call home? In the 1950s, Florida's image combined images of eternal sunshine and an innocence defined by tourism and leisure. Recently, Florida's image has been punctured by killer hurricanes, ballot-chasing lawyers, lurid crime, and alien exotics. Italian Americans may find new retirement centers in the South and West, places without the negative baggage of Florida.

But one should never underestimate the lure of the Florida Dream. For centuries, Italian immigrants and their children have been captivated by Florida. The Sunshine State, like few others, has the capacity to reinvent itself. A century ago, immigrants found new opportunities in this largely underdeveloped, under-populated state. Later, Italians capitalized upon Florida's image as the American Mediterranean. After World War II, Florida seduced a new generation with its powers of restoration and rejeuvenation. The dream endures.

It is highly fitting that at the dawn of a new millennium, Italians have completed their historic trajectory that started with the year of discovery.

The End

Bibliography

Books

Bailyn, Bernard. *Peopling of North America*. New York: Vintage Books, 1988.

Chester, Winston. *"Full Box": The Legendary Stories of the Men Who Built an Industry*. Panama City: Water P, 2001.

Dodson, Pat, ed. *Journey Through the Everglades: The Log of the Minnechana*. Tampa: Trend House, 1971.

Eidse, Faith, ed. *Voices of the Apalachicola*. Gainesville, FL: UP of Florida, 2006.

Gannon, Michael. *Rebel Bishop: Augustin Verot, Florida's Civil War Prelate*. Gainesville: UP of Florida, 1964.

Griffin, Patricia. *Mullet on the Beach: Minorcans in Florida, 1768–1785*. Gainesville: U of North Florida P, 1991.

McCalister, Lyle N. *Spain & Portugal in the New World: 1492–1700*. Minneapolis: U of Minnesota P, 1984.

McNally, Michael J. *Catholic Parish Life on Florida's West Coast, 1860–1968*. Catholic Media Ministries, Inc. 1996.

Mennillo, Anthony. *Arturo's Studio Presents Fort Walton Beach*. Freeport: Arturo's Studio, 2000.

Mennillo, Arturo. *Destin, Florida, Highway to Heaven: Vintage Photography by Arturo Mennillo*. Freeport: Arturo's Studio, 1988.

Milanich, Jerald T. *Frolicking Bears, Wet Vultures, & Other Oddities: A New York City Journalist in Nineteeth-Century Florida*. Gainesville: UP of Florida, 2005.

Mormino, Gary R. *Hillsborough County Goes to War: 1940–1950*. Tampa: Tampa Bay History Center, 2001.

Mormino, Gary R., and George E. Pozzetta. *The Immigrant World of Ybor City: Latins and Their Latin Neighbors in Tampa, Florida*. Urbana, IL: U of Illinois P, 1987.

Moroni, G. "L'Emigrazione Italiana in Florida." *Bolletino dell'Emigrazione* 1 (1915): 40.

Muir, Helen. *Miami, U.S.A.* Gainesville, FL: UP of Florida, 2000 ed.

O'Brien, Dawn, and Becky Matkov. *Florida's Historic Restaurants and Their Recipes*. Tampa: John F. Blair P, 1994.

Ortiz, Paul. *Emancipation Betrayed.* Berkeley: U of California P, 2005.

Pernetti, Nino and Ferdie Pacheco. *Nino Pernetti's Caffe Abbracci.* Gainesville: UP of Florida, 2008.

Pizzo, Anthony. *Tampa Town, 1824–1886: Cracker Village with a Latin Accent.* Tampa: Trend House, 1968.

Quinn, Jane. *Catholics of Marion County.* Ocala: Mission P, 1978.

Rasico, Phil D. *The Minorcans of Florida: Their History, Language and Culture.* New Smyrna Beach, FL: 1990.

Reid, Thomas. *America's Fortress: A History of Fort Jefferson, Dry Tortugas, Florida.* Gainesville: UP of Florida, 2006.

Rosasco-Soule, Adelia. *Panhandle Memories: A Lived History.* Pensacola, FL: West Florida Literary Association, 1991.

Roselli, Bruno. *The Italians in Colonial Florida, 1513–1821.*

Rybezynski, Witold, and Laurie Olin. *Vizcaya: An American Villa and Its Makers.* Philadelphia: U of Pennsylvania P, 2007.

Shofner, Jerrell. *Nor Is It Over Yet: Reconstruction in Florida.* Gainesville: UP of Florida, 1974.

Terkel, Studs. *The Good War: An Oral History of World War Two.* New York: Pantheon Books, 1984.

Urso, Frank. *A Stranger in the Barrio: Memoirs of a Tampa Sicilian.* Lincoln, NE: iUniverse, 2005.

Vickers, Elizabeth D. *We Will Have Music: The Story of the Greater Pensacola Symphony Orchestra.* Pensacola: Pensacola Historic Photographs, 2000.

Weeks, David. *Ringling: The Florida Years, 1911–1936.* Gainesville: UP of Florida, 1993.

Westfall, Loy Glenn. *Marti City: Florida's Ghost Town.* Key West: Key West Cigar City USA, 2000.

Willis, Elaine, Epggy Toifel, and Lea Wolf. *We Remember Bagdad.* Bagdad, FL: Bagdad Village Preservation Assoc., 1992.

Articles and Non-Published Materials

"A Chip Off the Italian Ice Block." *Naples Daily News* 11 June 2008.

"A Haven for Artists: Sarasota Colony." *Orlando Sentinel* 10 Dec. 2000.

"Al Bellotto, Rancher." *Lakeland Ledger* 29 Jan. 2001.

"At the Italian Club Cemetery." *St. Petersburg Times* 6 July 2008.

"*Brian's Song* Told the World about Brian Piccolo." *Sun-Sentinel* 1 Jan. 2007.

"Broward Political Kingmaker 'Trinchi' Trinchitella Dead." *South Florida Sun-Sentinel* 5 Feb. 2005.

"Citrus Cashes in on Growth." *Orlando Sentinel* 29 Mar. 1998.

"City Lacks Ethnic Enclaves." *Jacksonville Florida-Times Union* 24 Feb. 1996.

Cohen, Kathleen. "Immigrant Jacksonville: A Profile of Immigrant Groups in Jacksonville, Florida. 1890–1920." MA thesis, University of Florida, 1986.

"Con Colleano, Cirsus Performer." *St. Petersburg Times* 16 Nov. 1973.

"Dante Fascell." *New York Times* 1 Dec. 1998.

"Developer Views Yeehaw Junction." *Tampa Tribune* 23 Oct. 2006.

"'Everyone Turns Out to Be Something.'" *Tampa Tribune* 8 Dec. 2008.

"For Mama Gilda." *Palm Beach Post* 20 Sept. 2006.

"Frank Morsani." *Tampa Tribune* 11 Mar. 1984.

"Generoso Pope Jr. Dead at 61." *New York Times* 3 Oct. 1988.

"He Was Capone's Son." *South Florida History* 36 (2008): 12–13.

"His Life Was Like One of His Burgers." *St. Petersburg Times* 28 May 2008.

"If This House Could Talk." *Miami Herald* 2 Apr. 2006.

"In the Shadow of the Giant." *St. Petersburg Times* 12 Oct. 2005.

"Italian Heritage." *Palm Beach Post* 7 Nov. 1971.

"Italian Women Give Ludicrous Exhibition." *Tampa Morning Tribune* 15 Nov. 1910.

"Italian-American Lodge." *Miami Herald* 6 June 2004.

"Jerry Chiccone Sr. Built Citrus Empire." *Orlando Sentinel* 8 May 1998.

"John Sacino." *St. Petersburg Times* 27 May 1985.

"Judy Canova Dies." *New York Times* 7 Aug. 1983.

"King of the Court." *St. Petersburg Times* 25 Feb. 2007.

Knetsch, Joe. "The Peonage Controversy and the Florida East Coast Railway." *Tequesta* 59 (1999): 5–29.

"La colonia italiana di Tampa." *Bolletino dell'Emigrazione* (1927): 1237.

"Last Fish Monger." *St. Petersburg Times* 7 Dec. 2002.

"Let's Play, Name That Real Estate Project." *Port Charlotte Sun* 25 May 2006.

"Luccio Cristiani." *Sarasota-Herald Tribune* 24 Jan. 1992.

"Made by Momma." *St. Petersburg Times* 6 Dec. 2006.

"Market Offers Taste of Italy." *South Florida Business Journal* 2 Dec. 2005.

"Nova President Marking 10 Years." *South Florida Sun Sentinel* 8 June 2008.

Pacetti, Derald Jr. "Shrimping at Fernandina, Florida before 1920." Master's thesis, University of Florida, 1980.

Pozzetta, George. "A Padrone Looks at Florida: Labor Recruiting and the Florida East Coast Railway." *Florida Historical Quarterly* 54 (July 1975): 74–84.

"Still Having a Blast." *Miami Herald* 7 July 2007.

"Tampa Italians Urge Friends to Oust Reds." *Tampa Times* 1 Apr. 1948.

"Tampan Lands on Sicily and Meets His Kin." *Tampa Morning Tribune* 19 Aug. 1943.

"Tampans Love Their Spaghetti." *Tampa Tribune* 4 Apr. 1937.

"Tomato Turmoil." *Miami Herald* 28 Feb. 2008.

"Tony Leaves a Void Downtown Progress Can't Fill." *St. Petersburg Times* 24 Nov. 1980.

"Tribute to Steve Mondello." *Pensacola News-Journal* 20 Jan. 2007.

"Venettozzi Was Music's High Note." *Pensacola News-Journal* 28 Mar. 2006.

"Versaggi: Story is Florida Shrimping Saga." *Florida Times-Union* 30 Oct. 1960.

"Wally Schirra Dies." *Orlando Sentinel* 4 May 2007.

"War Brides." *Pensacola News-Journal* 2 July 1986.

"Woman's Cookbook Gives New Life to Traditional Italian Cooking." *Palm Beach Post* 18 Aug. 2004.

"Yeehaw's Destiny Awaits." *Tampa Tribune* 4 June 2006.

Government Documents
Archivio Comunale, Santo Stefano, Provincia di Agrigento, Italy.
US Censuses, 1870–2000.

Index

About the Author

Gary R. Mormino, a native of Wood River, Illinois, moved to Florida in 1977. Following his PhD at the University of North Carolina, he began teaching at the University of South Florida in Tampa.

Gary Mormino has published extensively on Italian Americana. His first book, *Immigrants on the Hill* (University of Illinois Press, 1986), dealt with the Hill, a famous Italian community in St. Louis, Missouri. In 1987, he co-authored (with George Pozzetta) *The Immigrant World of Ybor City* (University of Illinois Press, 1987). In 2005, he published *Land of Sunshine, State of Dreams: A Social History of Modern Florida.*

Mormino's teaching experience includes a Fulbright professorship to Italy, appointments to the Florida State University Study Center in Florence, Italy, and a fellowship at the Rockefeller Center in Bellagio, Italy. Presently, he holds the Frank E. Duckwall Professorship at the University of South Florida, St. Petersburg, where he is also the director of the Florida Studies Program.

VIA FOLIOS

A refereed book series dedicated to Italian studies and the culture
of Italian Americans in North America.

JOSEPH RICAPITO
Second Wave
Vol. 52, Poetry, $12.00

GARY MORMINO
Italians in Florida
Vol. 51, History, $15.00

GIANFRANCO ANGELUCCI
Federico F.
Vol. 50, Fiction, $16.00

ANTHONY VALERIO
The Little Sailor
Vol. 49, Memoir, $9.00

ROSS TALARICO
The Reptilian Interludes
Vol. 48, Poetry, $15.00

RACHEL GUIDO DEVRIES
Teeny Tiny Tino
Vol. 47, Children's Lit., $6.00

EMANUEL DIPASQUALE
Writing Anew
Vol. 46, Poetry, $15.00

MARIA FAMÀ
Looking for Cover
Vol. 45, Poetry, $15.00
CD, $6.00

ANTHONY VALERIO
Tony Cade Bambara's One Sicilian Night
Vol. 44, Memoir, $10.00

EMANUEL CARNEVALI
DENNIS BARONE, ED. & AFTERWORD
Furnished Rooms
Vol. 43, Poetry, $14.00

BRENT ADKINS, ET.AL
Shifting Borders
Vol. 42, Cultural Criticism, $18.00

GEORGE GUIDA
Low Italian
Vol. 41, Poetry, $11.00

GARDAPHÉ, GIORDANO, AND TAMBURRI
Introducing Italian Americana: Generalities on Literature and Film
Vol. 40, Criticism $10.00

DANIELA GIOSEFFI
Blood Autumn/Autunno di sangue
Vol. 39, Poetry, $15.00/$25.00

FRED MISURELLA
Lies to Live by
Vol. 38, Stories, $15.00

STEVEN BELLUSCIO
Constructing a Bibliography
Vol. 37, Italian Americana, $15.00

ANTHONY JULIAN TAMBURRI, ED.
Italian Cultural Studies 2002
Vol. 36, Essays, $18.00

BEA TUSIANI
con amore
Vol. 35, Memoir, $19.00

FLAVIA BRIZIO-SKOV, ED.
Reconstructing Societies in the Aftermath of War
Vol. 34, History/Cultural Studies, $30.00

A.J. TAMBURRI et al
Italian Cultural Studies 2001
Vol. 33, Essays, $18.00

ELIZABETH GIOVANNAMESSINA, ED.
In Our Own Voices
Vol. 32, Ital. Amer. Studies, $25.00

STANISLAO G. PUGLIESE
Desperate Inscriptions
Vol. 31, History, $12.00

HOSTERT & TAMBURRI, EDS.
Screening Ethnicity
Vol. 30, Ital. Amer. Culture, $25.00

G. PARATI & B. LAWTON, EDS.
Italian Cultural Studies
Vol. 29, Essays, $18.00

HELEN BAROLINI
More Italian Hours & Other Stories
Vol. 28, Fiction, $16.00

FRANCO NASI, ed.
Intorno alla Via Emilia
Vol. 27, Culture, $16.00

ARTHUR L. CLEMENTS
The Book of Madness and Love
Vol. 26, Poetry, $10.00

Published by BORDIGHERA, INC., an independently owned not-for-profit scholarly organization that has no legal affiliation to the University of Central Florida or John D. Calandra Italian American Institute, Queens College/CUNY.

www.ingramcontent.com/pod-product-compliance
Lightning Source LLC
Chambersburg PA
CBHW052209270326
41931CB00011B/2284

9 781884 419973